1599   Moved to Southwark near the Globe Theatre which he and his company had recently erected.

1602   Extensive purchases of property and land in Stratford.

1602–4   Lodged with Mountjoy, a Huguenot refugee and a maker of headdresses, in Cripplegate, London. Helped to arrange a marriage between Mary Mountjoy and Stephen Belott, her father's apprentice.

1603   His company became the King's Majesty's Players under royal patronage.

1607   His daughter Susanna married Dr John Hall.

1608   Birth of Shakespeare's grand-daughter Elizabeth Hall.

1610   Shakespeare possibly returned to live in Stratford.

1613   Purchase of the Gatehouse in Blackfriars. Burning of the Globe Theatre during the première of *Henry VIII*.

1616   Marriage of his daughter Judith to Thomas Quiney in Lent for which they were excommunicated.

25 March, 1616   Shakespeare altered the draft of his will presumably to give Judith more security in view of her husband's unreliability and his pre-marital misconduct with another woman. His will also revealed his strong attachment to his Stratford friends, and above all his desire to arrange for the establishment of his descendants.

23 April, 1616   Death of Shakespeare.

1623   Publication of the First Folio edition of Shakespeare's plays collected by his fellow actors Heminge and Condell to preserve 'the memory of so worthy a friend'.

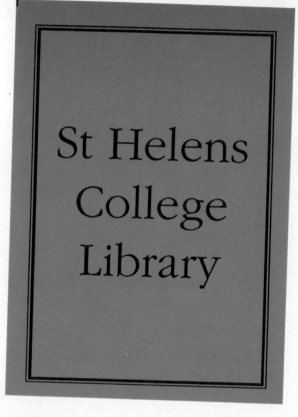

THE PLAYERS' SHAKESPEARE

KING HENRY V

The Players' Shakespeare

MACBETH

TWELFTH NIGHT

THE MERCHANT OF VENICE

KING HENRY IV PART ONE

JULIUS CÆSAR

A MIDSUMMER NIGHT'S DREAM

AS YOU LIKE IT

THE TEMPEST –

ROMEO AND JULIET

ANTONY AND CLEOPATRA

HAMLET

OTHELLO

RICHARD II

Also edited by Dr J. H. Walter

HENRY V (Arden Shakespeare)

CHARLEMAGNE (Malone Society)

LAUNCHING OF THE MARY (Malone Society)

KING HENRY V

Edited by
J. H. WALTER

M.A., PH.D.

Formerly Headmaster
Minchenden School, Southgate
Fellow of University College, London

HEINEMANN
EDUCATIONAL

Heinemann Educational Books Ltd
Halley Court, Jordan Hill, Oxford OX2 8EJ
OXFORD LONDON EDINBURGH
MADRID ATHENS BOLOGNA PARIS
MELBOURNE SYDNEY AUCKLAND
IBADAN NAIROBI HARARE GABORONE
SINGAPORE TOKYO PORTSMOUTH NH (USA)

ISBN 0 435 19008 3

© J. H. WALTER 1967

FIRST PUBLISHED 1967

92 93 94 95 96 13 12 11 10 9 8 7 6 5 4

Printed in England by Clays Ltd, St Ives plc

CONTENTS

PREFACE   *page* 1

INTRODUCTION   3

KING HENRY V   26

APPENDICES:

  I Sources   243

  II Shakespeare's Theatre   244

PREFACE

THE aim of this edition is to encourage pupils to study the play as a play, to see it not so much as a novel or a historical narrative, but as a pattern of speech and movement creating an artistic whole. This approach stimulates and enlivens classroom work and is also a most fruitful way of preparing for examinations.

The interleaved notes, therefore, contain, in addition to a gloss, interpretations of character, dialogue and imagery, considered particularly from the point of view of a play. There are some suggestions for acting, for the most part simple pointers to avoid rigidity of interpretation and drawn up with an apron stage in mind. Some questions are interposed to provide topics for discussion or to assist in discrimination.

It is suggested that the play should be read through rapidly with as little comment as possible. On a second reading the notes should be used in detail, and appropriate sections of the Introduction might be read at the teacher's discretion.

It is hoped that this edition will enable the teacher to take his class more deeply into the play than the usual meagre allowance of time permits him to do; it is not an attempt to usurp his function.

The Folio (1623) text here printed is complete. No attempt has been made to discuss the issues raised by possible revisions of the play, the promise in the Epilogue to *2 Henry IV* 'to continue the story with Sir John (i.e. Falstaff) in it', or with the theories of the provenance of the Folio text. For these matters the reader is referred to the present editor's Arden (1960) edition.

The modern editions of P. Alexander, C. J. Sisson, J. Dover Wilson have been freely and gratefully consulted. Stage directions follow in the main those of the Folio. Suggested locations of scenes have been placed in the notes.

From among the many modern general works and studies of the play I am particularly indebted to the following: Lily B. Campbell, *Shakespeare's Histories*; H. C. Goddard, *The Meaning of Shakespeare*; P. Jorgensen,

Preface

Shakespeare's Military World; L. C. Knights, *Shakespeare: The Histories*; H. M. V. Matthews, *Character and Symbol in Shakespeare's Plays*; M. M. Reese, *The Cease of Majesty*; I. Ribner, *The English History Play in the Age of Shakespeare*; E. M. W. Tillyard, *Shakespeare's History Plays*; D. Traversi, *Shakespeare from Richard II to Henry V*.

Similarly I am indebted to articles by R. W. Battenhouse, S. Berman, S. L. Bethell, A. Gilbert, P. Jorgensen, W. M. Merchant, E. C. Pettet, L. J. Ross, Z. Stribrny, Rose Zimbardo.

J.H.W.

INTRODUCTION

I

DATE AND PERFORMANCE

I T seems certain that the lines in the Chorus to Act V,

> Were now the general of our gracious Empress,
> As in good time he may, from Ireland coming,
> Bringing rebellion broached on his sword,

refer to the Earl of Essex, who left London on 27 March, 1599 with an army to crush Tyrone's rebellion, and who returned in September without success. The play then was written sometime between March and September 1599. This receives some support from the fact that Francis Meres does not mention the play in the lists he published in *Palladis Tamia*, September/October 1598, though his lists are incomplete. A quarto edition appeared in 1600 apparently put together by one or two members of the company—perhaps the actors who played Exeter and Gower—from a version of the play shortened for touring in the country. Reprints of this quarto appeared in 1602 and 1619. The Folio version which is the basis of this text appeared in 1623. There is no record of the play's production, apart from the mention on the title page of the Quarto that it had been 'sundry times played by . . . the Lord Chamberlain his servants', until 7 January, 1605 when it was performed at Court. Presumably it then made full use of all the magnificent and lavish scenic devices, properties, and costumes of the Revels Office.

3

II

CRITICAL OPINIONS

Criticism of *Henry V* is much confused. There has been condemnation of the play's structure as a 'thing of shreds and
patches', and of Henry as a 'strutting rhetorician' and a hypocrite.
Some have seen Henry as the 'mirror of christian kings', others
as the subtle politician, the cold efficient man. To account for
the defects which many see in the play it has been held that
Shakespeare was hampered by the historical and legendary
material which was impossible to treat dramatically. Traversi
considered that the idea of the successful king contained con-
tradictions within itself which come to the surface in the play.
Goddard saw in the portrait of Henry as the ideal king only
iconoclastic irony which reveals the machiavellian prince, though
astonishingly he admits that the audience would not notice this
in the performance. Battenhouse claimed that Shakespeare
debunked military glory by investing the incidents and characters
in the play with satirical edge and ironical overtones.

Whatever validity the last two criticisms may have is weakened
by their reliance on matters not in the play at all, but found only
in Holinshed and *2 Henry IV*, by the avoidance of incidents
incapable of satire or irony, by misreadings of the text, and by
distorted analogies. Indeed one implication of their reading of
Shakespeare's views has eluded them. There is no evidence in
his plays that Shakespeare did not accept the common Elizabethan view that God was the arbiter of victories. If he did so
accept this view then the assertion that Henry's alleged fraudulent
piety deceived God into granting him the victory is in Elizabethan
eyes as pretty a piece of blasphemy as ever slipped by the censor-
ship of the Master of Revels.

The difficulties that some critics find in accepting the play
arise chiefly from the essentially modern suppositions on which
they base their views. They assume among other things that war

4

is a crime caused by man's actions alone, that military glory is therefore hollow, that formal oratory is either ridiculous, strained or 'phoney', and that openly expressed piety is a sign of hypocrisy or of a guilty conscience. But Shakespeare in this play appears to subscribe to none of these things. Again a play, it is asserted, should have dramatic conflict and inner tensions, but in the episodic pageant-like acts of *Henry V* these are not notably present. In short on the grounds of themes, moral concepts, style, and structure the play fails. Yet at the time of writing *Henry V* Shakespeare was at the height of his powers and unlikely to make a bad play. Therefore to resolve this dilemma critics have attempted to save Shakespeare's face by attributing to him two contradictory levels of writing.

III

SOME ELIZABETHAN CONCEPTS

Some help to see the play in perspective may be gained by examining the Elizabethan views on matters expressed in the play, since it is generally accepted that Shakespeare pondered carefully any material relevant to the themes of his plays, particularly of his historical plays.

The purpose of the writing of history for the Elizabethans was the religious one of displaying the unfolding of God's plan for mankind, the order, harmony, and correspondence throughout his universe, his justice and reason in the shifts of power and prosperity in kingdoms and in the risings and fallings of great men. This view was inherited by the history plays of the period from the morality plays. From other sources different concepts of history supplemented or even varied from this major purpose. History was seen as cyclical and repetitive, and hence its purpose was to provide models for guidance, or warning analogies to contemporary statesmen. It could also serve to glorify a nation. Something of each of these matters appears in *Henry V*.

History was also the subject matter for epic poetry. The form of the play with its invocation, its choruses and its theme indicates that Shakespeare was experimenting with epic conventions in drama in a most original way. The proper theme for epic poetry was held to be war, or sometimes war and peace. In form the epic should have unity, and its purpose was moral; it sought to teach by example, illustration, and sometimes by allegory. Love might be part of the action, but not the poetical courtly love which would lack decorum. The manner of writing included formal speeches, long similes, proverbs or 'sententiae', expressed in a high dignified style. Its hero should be of royal rank, divinely guided, and beyond ordinary men in virtue.

Shakespeare matched the epic hero with the ideal prince, another contemporary concept which had been discussed in numerous writings throughout the centuries. How closely Henry conforms to some of the qualities considered essential in the ideal prince may be seen in the following attributes selected from a very popular account by Erasmus. The prince should be a christian, an ardent supporter of the Church, and he should be learned in divinity. His kingdom should in its parts be as well ordered as the human body or as the obedient kingdom of the bees. He represents justice but should show mercy and not pervert justice for his own private revenge. He should keep himself under strict self-control and not give way to passions. At all times he should be guided by the advice of wise men. While affable with lowly people he should avoid being corrupted by them. He should defend and preserve his kingdom, the cares of which keep him awake at night. Some titles given to kings are mere flattery and to be rejected. Although it is fashionable to compare princes with heroes of antiquity, he should remember that as a christian he is far better than such men as Alexander. There are other lesser parallels.

Kings found themselves necessarily involved in war, and the conduct and morality of war were topics that evoked considerable discussion throughout the sixteenth century. The following abstract gives a fair picture of the consensus of opinion among writers such as Gates, Norden, and Sutcliffe, contemporaries of Shakespeare. Armies were founded with God's approval for the purpose of preserving society and for repressing and punishing sinful, rebellious mankind. Martial qualities ennobled and honoured a nation and were a sign that God sought to make it prosperous. God uses wars to execute justice and to wreak vengeance on sinners. Even the appalling savageries of murder, rape, injustice and sacrilege in war were 'God's salve' for wickedness. Wars were curative of the diseases that grew in peace-time, of the abuses of peace, of pride among nations. God alone decided who should win the victory. He decreed whether men should die in battle or not, neither their own skill nor their strength could decide that issue. A soldier's duty was to obey his officers without question whether the cause be just or unjust; obedience should be absolute and implicit. Soldiers should be advised of the justice of their cause. If the cause was unjust, responsibility rested on the king for the deaths of innocent people. Those who first offended gave cause for a just war against themselves by those who sought restitution. For example, the French so offended the Black Prince by rejecting his offers.

The leader of an army should be firm in his religion, should show mercy, prevent pillage, and give God the credit for victory. He should be alert enough to devise favourable interpretations of bad signs, he should by his speeches encourage his soldiers, he should be to his men the 'sun from whose beams every soldier borroweth his shine' (compare IV Chorus, 41–5). Before all enterprises he should commend his men and himself to God. With such a general 'an army may resemble the divine Image'. '. . . So shall there be seen that sweet comfort and heavenly harmony in their warfare, which shall gain the love, favour and affection of the heavenly company' (Norden).

IV

THE SHAPING OF THE PLAY WITHIN
ELIZABETHAN CONCEPTS

All these things provide groundwork for the play. The celebration of national glory and martial virtues fit in with Henry's qualities as the ideal king and epic hero. The epic style distances the play from the spectator, it provokes reflection and invites imaginary encounters and visual impressions. It allows for very little action on the stage, but much that is reported as having happened: Henry's conversion, and the deaths of Falstaff, York, and Suffolk; and some things that may happen: Henry's threats to Harfleur, the boasts of the French nobles. There is a council of war, a discussion about the responsibilities of a king and of his soldiers; there are varying descriptions of a traitor, a king's cares, despoiled France, the poor English army, the Dauphin's horse, as well as the interlinking choruses. What action there is, is limited to matters like the glove episode, the trapping of the traitors, the beating of Pistol, and the wooing of Kate.

It was in keeping with epic style that fearful battles should be rendered in the music of eloquent orderly rhetorical discourse and not in violence and disorder on the stage which might disturb the serenely ordered victory. Further, stage combats with all the indignities and shortcomings mentioned in IV Chorus, 49–52 might lower the heroic pitch, or alternatively attribute too much to the prowess of the individual and so fail to credit God alone with the victory. It may be for this reason that there is no mention of battle tactics, Henry's fight with Alençon, and the archers, but only of the 'plain shock and even play of battle'.

These epic patterns are thus embraced by the divine plan. The play is as it were founded in theology. The account of Henry's conversion in which Canterbury and Ely significantly acknowledge God's 'means How things are perfected' is based on St

Paul's doctrine of grace. Henry is now receiving God's grace, and henceforth through him as instrument God works out his purposes. Henry acknowledges God's aid in unmasking treason, and in granting him an astonishing victory; his frequent expressions of piety are reminders of this aid, they are natural enough and not humbug. Henry's prayer with its reference to the guilt of Richard II's death is another reminder of the pattern. In the wooing scene Henry expresses a wish for a son that will fight for Christendom against the Turks. The irony is not the usual dramatic kind, but is related to the divine ordering of things, and it serves to remind the audience of that order. The epilogue arranged in the form of a sonnet makes the point of the play precisely and clearly. In the first eight lines Henry the 'star of England' is celebrated; the last six lines recall the disasters that followed in the reign of his son because many regents broke its unity.

Again the divine pattern of the diverse universe with its order, harmony, and unity has its correspondences throughout the play. The description of Henry's conversion proclaims him at one within himself, he has now no strife within the soul. Exeter and Canterbury describe the harmony of a kingdom and divine ordering of the state of man. Canterbury's account of the idealized society of the bees where varied occupations are directed to one end is a comparison with Henry's government of England. Harmony and obedience are apparently complete except for the treason that comes to light, but this is inspired by the French, who are depicted as disordered and promoters of disorder throughout the play. At the lowest level even the quarrels of Pistol and Nym are resolved by the peace-making of Bardolph and the prospect of loot in France. That prime mover of disorder Falstaff is gently led to 'Arthur's bosom'. The four captains with their diversity of tongues are united in their application to the techniques of warfare, and the accomplishment of the work in hand whatever fun their accents and parody of a topical debate

9

may provide. Even the language lesson is directed toward the end of unity by marriage.

Henry's presence among his soldiers 'mean and gentle all' gathers them together in a unity of spirit while Fluellen insists on the maintenance of strict external order and discipline. Despite their unease the soldiers are united in their loyalty to Henry. Even the deaths of York and Suffolk are described as being in harmony with man and their maker.

By contrast the French are at odds. They disagree in their estimate of Henry, they are undecided and hesitant over bringing Henry to battle, and they squabble without settling their personal animosities. Their disorder in battle and lack of leadership plunge them into the further disorder of neglecting military rules, killing the non-combatant boys and lackeys, and forcing Henry to make the unpleasant decision to kill his prisoners.

In the final scene Burgundy makes a powerful plea for the return of orderly peace to the countryside of France, a plea which is echoed in Queen Isabel's prayer for the unity of 'hearts in one, your realms in one'.

Henry himself is the central inspirer of order, and all things in the play have reference to him and reflect aspects of his virtue.

V

HENRY

Undoubtedly the Elizabethans saw in Henry a figure of national glory, probably the greatest of English kings, the closest to their concept of the ideal prince, and an emblem of epic qualities. In the play he is carefully drawn, but is he anything more than a bare artefact, a pastiche of political virtuosity and piety? To see him as a man where 'all his senses have but human conditions' is made difficult by Henry's extraordinary self-control and the elegant rhetorical form of his speeches. Yet within the

patterned rhetoric of his denunciation of Scroop, the bosom
friend who betrayed him, there are the undertones of bitterness
held in severe restraint. The eve of Agincourt reveals Henry's
human touch. His army appears doomed, he might well despair,
yet in disguise he visits his soldiers. He endures Pistol's insult
with patience, tries to remove the doubtful mood of the three
soldiers not only by explanations but by the relish of a challenge
to be met. The strain and tension on Henry are considerable; he
accepts the responsibilities of his throne and the inheritance of
his father's guilt for which God's vengeance is inevitable. For
all he knows that vengeance may be wreaked on him by defeat
and death in the battle to come. Yet his courage and inner harmony
give him poise enough to greet his troops with the moving
Crispin speech, and to crack a grim jest with Montjoy. There
is exhilaration in his approach to the fight against overwhelming
odds, the kind of fight that men find deeply stirring. Something
of the quality 'terrible in constant resolution' noted by the
Constable shows in his order to kill the prisoners. The practical
joke that completes the glove episode is a rough geniality wholly
acceptable in soldierly company. Henry woos with zest and
gaiety, and quick perceptiveness, but his emotions are under
control, no unruly, disordered passion drives him into 'sighing
like furnace' or composing sonnets to Kate.

Henry has things in common with Prospero. There is something
absolute about both, both appear to lack inner conflict, as both
plays appear to lack dramatic tension. Henry is the noble warrior
king creating by military force a unified state within the fixed
bounds of history; Prospero is the philosopher-king creating by
the force of magical power an ideal state outside history, but
both states are subject to mutability.

Henry operates within the frame of christian doctrines that
have become obscure, and within political and philosophical
assumptions that are obsolete, but which surprisingly recur.
Even if some find the logic of the play terrifying in its compli-

cations, yet there is sufficient in the play that is universal in its appeal, and that seizes the imagination and catches at the heart.

VI

OTHER CHARACTERS

The English nobles are not clearly differentiated although Exeter shows some hearty robust directness as ambassador, and some sensitivity in his account of the deaths of York and Suffolk. It may be that their characters were levelled down so that nothing should detract from Henry's greatness.

The French nobles have more marked characteristics. The Dauphin is immature, spoilt, full of prejudices, lacking a sense of proportion, and pathetically apt to propose ill-considered courses of action. Orleans is his loyal supporter against the elderly censorious Constable. There is indecision and lack of leadership in their councils but no lack of courage. The Dauphin for example achieves his wish to fight at Agincourt in spite of his father's prohibition. There is no sign of leadership, no martial discipline or order, no forethought, even the Constable's guidon is not ready when it should be. Their preparation for battle consists of boasting of their armour and horses, some bawdy jesting, malicious comments about the Dauphin's courage, and bragging of their forthcoming achievements against the English. Unlike the latter they make no spiritual preparation for death.

Fluellen is in some ways a curious reflection of Henry himself with his insistence on order and discipline, his refusal to interfere with the course of justice, his round of stations at night, his Welshness, and his taking Henry's place in the glove episode. In part he is a keeper of Henry's conscience as well as the precise executant of his orders. He is pedantically interested in military disciplines derived from the practice of classical generals, but his enthusiasm prevents him from becoming a bore. His earnestness, touchiness, and his lack of humour might not recommend him, but his pride in his work, his overflowing pluralities in his speech, and his devoted love for Henry are endearing. With delicious, patronizing uprightness he gravely announces that he need not be ashamed of Henry as long as he is an honest man. He promptly pins Henry down over his affair with Williams, but Henry turns the tables by making him his proxy to receive the payment of a box in the ears. It is appropriately given to him forcibly to remove the irregular discord Pistol from the order and harmony of those who fought on Crispin's day.

To Pistol and Bardolph, the 'irregular humorists' of *2 Henry IV* is added a third disturber of civil order, Nym. Pistol who has married Nell Quickly in spite of her promise to marry Nym and her anticipations of becoming Lady Falstaff, is a boastful, swaggering, cowardly soldier of a type that appeared in earlier comedies both English and continental. Jorgensen saw irony in his rank as 'ancient' for it was a post demanding high courage; perhaps it was self-conferred. His name has some aptness for the pistol was noted for the violence and unpredictability of its detonation and the uncertainty of its aim. There are traces of parody in Pistol's activities. Like mock knights he and Nym have quarrelled over the favours of Mistress Quickly, a bawd, but Bardolph's resolution, their cowardice, and the prospect of pickings in the war in France settle the dispute and unite them in a dishonourable brotherhood of thieves.

Pistol is full of sound and fury, but he rapidly retreats from danger behind a smoke screen of verbiage. His curious sing-song verse (he always speaks in verse) old-fashioned in its alliterations, and his occasional classical allusion, mock his pretensions. His attempts at a ceremonious and dignified high style with his impersonal statements, 'fury shall abate', 'profits will accrue', and his grammatical disorders 'I thee command', 'I will some mercy show', render him ridiculous. He imitates the bombast of earlier Elizabethan tragedies and in his own imagination he is 'As good a gentleman as the Emperor'.

His bluster deceives Fluellen and the French soldier, ironically named le Fer (sword), who is bullied in a travesty of ransoming practice. Fluellen's disciplinary cudgel drives him from the honourable company of Agincourt to dishonourable desertion and degrading livelihood. It is curious that he alone of the humorists is allowed to survive. Does he represent something perpetual, the iniquity that always survives, or is it the worst punishment for Pistol to go on living out his cowardice and his evil?

Some have interpreted the words and activities of Pistol and his fellows at Harfleur as a satire on Henry's preceding speech, and have alleged similar satirical parallels elsewhere. But Shakespeare's practice of making sub-plots and episodes parallel with main plot and episodes is not normally for satirical purposes which Shakespeare sets out directly, but is a device for enhancing the main plot by the difference.

Nym is a mutterer of dark threats through vague, bloodthirsty innuendoes, yet he is a man of few words and fewer deeds. He shrugs off discussion with his humour-phrase, 'that's the humour of it', or with a fatalistic appeal to the way things are. His short, clipped, obscure, repetitive speech reveals his limited intelligence. Some have seen in the squabble between Pistol and Nym a topical hit at Ben Jonson and Marston, playwrights of the time. But Nym stands for some of the vices that attach themselves to armies. Thence the discipline of Fluellen drives him on in a cloud of bad humours to his obscure death.

Bardolph appears as a peace-maker between Nym and Pistol, remembering Falstaff with some loyalty and affection and not, one hopes, merely as the provider of fuel for the fire in his face. His death for sacrilege is reported to Henry who approves.

These knaves have no share in honour, their motives were unjust, they were disturbers of right order, and they are swept away.

The Boy, Falstaff's page, has something of the impudence

and quick-wittedness of Moth in *Love's Labour's Lost*. He is the mouthpiece for incisive comment on the cowardice and crime of his companions. His attempt to free himself from their corruption is cut short by his death. His death heralded by his own comment in the unchivalrous French attack on the boys and the lackeys adds an edge to Fluellen's disgust and indignation.

Katharine is frank, intelligent, modest and has a demure sense of fun. Her liveliness matches Henry's, and she fences delicately with him, manoeuvring him into committing himself to speak in French so that he woos her on terms of her own choosing. Even though she teases him, she retains perfect courtesy, and her acceptance of Henry is graceful and dignified.

VII

STAGE CONDITIONS AND THE PLAY

The stage conditions described in Appendix II determined to a large extent the shape of the plays, their dramatic devices, and their methods and conventions.

The staging of *Henry V* begins with council chamber scenes, the two scenes before the Boar's Head tavern, and further council scenes. In Act III the stage is set for a siege. For the walls or battlements of Harfleur the balcony may have been used, and soldiers bore the scaling ladders mentioned in the Folio stage direction. Act IV, during which many hours elapse, contains camp and battle scenes. No combat episodes occur, in fact all the scenes could be arranged in the front of tents, or even with no properties at all. Act V begins with a camp scene and ends with the final palace scene. All the scenes are in due chronological sequence, though the Quarto edition places IV. iv after IV. v, an arrangement which has much to commend it.

As usual acts and scenes are not introduced with any statement of where they take place. The precise locating of every scene would distract attention from the plot; the scene is where the actors are. Such imprecision coupled with the uninterrupted flow of the play helps to maintain the dramatic illusion. In *Henry V* the stage direction in the Folio, 'scaling ladders at Harfleur' (III. i) is perhaps the book-keeper's note for properties required which has crept into print. II. i is placed somewhere in London, it is not fully clear whether it is an indoor or an outdoor scene.

A marked difference between this play and Shakespeare's other plays, except *Pericles*, is the use of a chorus at the beginning of every act. Its function here is to invite imaginative visual re-creation of some historic episodes omitted from the play, to pre-set the forthcoming scenes, to conjure up and intensify relevant attitudes among the spectators, and to bridge over the gaps in time and thus preserve some semblance of unity. It also detached and distanced the play from the spectators setting its epic story apart for reverential admiration and wonder beyond the intimate personal involvement of the spectator.

An important convention was the use of the soliloquy and the aside. The jutting out of the stage into the middle of the theatre floor brought the actors who were well forward nearer to the bulk of the audience than to actors at the rear of the stage. It had long been established that character and motives were announced directly, the audience was not left to guess what was going on in a character's mind. It was a simple matter, therefore, for an actor to come forward out of earshot of the others on the stage and reveal confidentially to the audience his character, his motives, and his intentions. In this way Shylock and Richard III declare their villainy, Prince Hal his intention to give up his bad companions, and Olivia her love for Viola. This device linked actor and audience intimately: the spectators shared in the play, they had a god-like knowledge of the hearts of the characters, and the two things were used to increase their feelings of tension and suspense, and the moments of dramatic irony. The aside, a brief pointed remark, is often ironic, or it may give the audience a kind of nudge to remind them of some matter. It too sustains the sense of intimacy between actor and audience.

Soliloquies in *Henry V* are limited to Henry, the Boy, and Pistol. Pistol's confession of his evil intentions subsequent to the play is in the convention of the villain, this time defeated but prepared to renew his villainy in another form. The Boy's two soliloquies are different. The first (III. ii, 25–47) reveals the cowardice and thievery of Pistol, Bardolph, and Nym, and only briefly his own desire to leave their company. The second (IV. iv, 64–72) denounces Pistol's cowardice, mentions the deaths of Nym and Bardolph, and adds a remark that anticipates his own death. In neither of these is the audience intimately involved.

Henry's soliloquies too are not confessions and intimacies shared with the audience. He complains of the burdensome responsibilities of kingship in a kind of self-communing on which the audience may eavesdrop but not share. Similarly the audience cannot share the private meditation of his prayer.

It is significantly in keeping with the dignity of the story that there are no asides.

Elizabethan military costume and accoutrements would presumably have been worn. In V. ii magnificent court dresses would have given rich, spectacular pageantry.

VIII

VERSE AND PROSE

The impact of dialogue was enhanced by its traditional verse form; it gave to the major characters an impressive grandeur, a stature larger than life. In Shakespeare's plays its range, power, and flexibility are truly astounding. In addition he uses prose which is almost as varied in style and force.

Shakespeare's verse is infinitely varied. He uses heroic couplets to form a stately narrative verse in *Richard II*, or two speakers can each speak a line of a couplet, the second speaker making a

comment on the first (*A Midsummer Night's Dream*, I. i, 194–201).
A few couplets appearing in blank verse may mark an intense
emotion; a single couplet may mark a wise or significant saying,
or an important exit. Couplets can impart a sense of finality, of
steps taken from which there can be no turning back. Couplets
of shorter lines, however, are often mocking jingles (*Merchant of
Venice*, I. i, 111–12) though they too can be impressively final (*A
Midsummer Night's Dream*, V. i, 405 ff.).

In early plays such as *Love's Labour's Lost* and *Romeo and Juliet*
Shakespeare used elaborate rhyme patterns. The first words
Romeo and Juliet speak to each other form the pattern of a sonnet.
Such patterns employed with elaborate figures of speech are a
sign of the depth and sincerity of the speakers' feelings. We are
inclined to regard them as artificial and insincere, but to an
Elizabethan they truly reflected the strength and complexity of
the emotion described. No such devices are used in this play.

Shakespeare's blank verse can be elaborate, enriched with
swiftly following metaphors, with similes and other figures of
speech or tricks of style, and with mythological allusions; it can
be plain and direct; or it can become exaggerated and violent in
language in the description of warfare, in frenzied appeals to the
heavens, and in boasting. Its rhythms can march with regular
beat, or, particularly in later plays like *King Lear* and *Antony and
Cleopatra*, the rhythms are infinitely varied to achieve the most
subtle effects. The characters may use the kind of blank verse
appropriate to the dramatic moment and not necessarily the kind
consistent with what is known of them elsewhere in the play.

In *Henry V* kings, prelates, nobles, heralds, and Pistol normally
speak in blank verse. There are some scenes and episodes however
where prose is the medium: Henry's discussion with his soldiers
on the eve of the battle, the bickering of the French nobles, Henry's
second meeting with Williams and its following conversation
with Fluellen, Henry's wooing and its concluding exchanges
with Burgundy and the French King. There is little rhyming

verse. Some scenes have exit couplets; only rarely are couplets introduced to emphasize a point (I. ii, 287–8; 295–6). Pistol's snatches of plainsong have rhymes, and the Epilogue is a sonnet.

These characters, except Pistol, all maintain a dignified level of speaking, their verse is orderly, even, untroubled by inter-jections of emotion. It is descriptive and persuasive, its images differentiated and not fused together, its rhythms deftly varied within limited wavelengths.

Canterbury, when he is not following Holinshed's investi-gations into the pedigrees of the French kings, has smooth, powerful, and richly allusive verse, organized in rhetorical patterns with precision. His changes of rhythm are subtle, effective, and never violent.

Henry's verse is more flexible and supple, not so ponderous as that of the prelates, swifter in tempo, its images generally directed to the dramatic situation, though some in his charges against Scroop and in his soliloquy on the 'hard condition' of a king are generalized. His longer speeches are well organized and efficient, formal rhetorical constructions are not so apparent except again in the two speeches just mentioned. His verse is discursive, directive, persuasive, argumentative, it is not broken by emotional outbursts or the struggle to express a divided mind.

Pistol's irregular blank verse parodies its speaker. It is inflated, stilted bombast. Its meaning is obscure if not hollow, its rhythms jerk and swagger, it is pestered with alliteration and tortured syntax. For the boastful soldier, the *miles gloriosus*, of ancient lineage, and elevated in his own conceit, verse of this pretentious kind is an apt way of exposing his emptiness.

Why the Epilogue should be cast in sonnet form is not clear. It is reasonable to suppose that the contrast between Henry, the 'star of England' in the octave and the succeeding disastrous multiple rule in the sestet gathers up and seals the play's theme of unity and order within the providential mutability of history.

The prose of this play is more varied than the blank verse.

Nym's short simple statements supported by repeated assertions of the inevitability of events and the predominance of his humours are signs of limited intelligence and restricted speech. The Hostess has simple linked sentences broken by exclamations, and in her account of Falstaff's death her speech takes on some of the rhythms of verse. Her garrulity defeats her apprehension and produces malapropisms and misunderstandings. In III. ii, the Boy in his witty analysis of the characters of Pistol, Bardolph, and Nym speaks with mature prose. He speaks with short direct statements clearly expressed and balanced by short incisive inferences varied by an occasional proverb.

Fluellen utters a delightful progression of plural nouns and singular verbs. His capacity for multiplying 'variations' and accumulating nouns and adjectives is prodigious. The whole is enlivened by such interjections as 'look you', 'I warrant you' and 'in my conscience'.

The French nobles conduct their eve of battle talk in prose instead of their normal blank verse. This may be to emphasize the trivial, demeaning nature of that conversation. As this scene is separated only by a chorus from Henry's prose talks with the soldiers, Shakespeare may have felt that if the French nobles spoke verse it might have dignified them unduly, and that Henry might suffer by comparison.

Henry speaks a deal of prose. His explanations to the soldiers are clear and forcible, at times strengthened by telling imagery and succinct proverb-like statements or definitions. Occasionally there are carefully phrased antitheses and paradoxes which sharpen the argument. His wooing speeches are more colloquial, lighter in texture, quickly changing direction, eloquent yet simple in sentence structure. It might be expected that a wooing scene would be conducted in verse, but Katharine's limited English, the misunderstandings that enliven the situation, and Henry's claim to be plain soldier scorning the writing of love poems may be sufficient reasons.

It is sometimes very difficult to understand why Shakespeare changes the dialogue from verse to prose or from one style of blank verse to another. Why, for example, does Montjoy use prose in III. vi, 110–26 and verse elsewhere? Occasionally the changes may be due to cuts, alterations or additions made to the original play, but in general the variations are deliberately designed to achieve some dramatic effect. They should not, therefore, be overlooked or lightly dismissed in study of the play.

IX

VOCABULARY, IMAGES, DEVICES OF STYLE

The play contains frequent words and images associated with animals, religion, warfare, and husbandry, of varying dramatic significance. Thus the first scene contains a large number of theological terms not only in the description of Henry's change of heart but elsewhere in the conversation of the two prelates. This serves to confirm the pious basis of Henry's character and actions, and creates in the audience a mood prepared to accept that the action of the play is strongly informed with religious attitudes.

No other play by Shakespeare has such a variety of accents— French, Welsh, Irish, Scottish, not to mention the Hostess' malapropisms, Pistol's malpractices with words and Nym's concessions to his humours. Perhaps like Henry with Kate all this broken English is to be accepted as forming one consort of broken music, or with Fluellen that they are 'a little variations' but essentially agree together in unity.

Words and phrases in this tautly constructed play are very frequently repeated sometimes with added associations ('bar', I. ii, 12, 35, 92, 94; 'chase', I. ii, 266; II. iv, 68; 'consent', I. ii, 181; II. ii, 22), sometimes to mark similar situations (I. ii, 108–10; II. iv, 57–62; I. ii, 112–14; III. i, 21; IV. ii, 23), sometimes as a retort ('savour', I. ii, 250, 295), and occasionally to underline a point of view or an attitude ('mock', 'mockeries', I. ii, 281–6; IV Chor. 53; IV. iii, 92; V. i, 50–63). There are other repetitions, perhaps fortuitous which yet help to brace the play more tightly.

Among the numerous metaphors, similes, and other figures of speech some are remarkably illuminating in their concentration of concrete and abstract:

> Picked from the worm-holes of long-vanished days,
> Nor from the dust of old oblivion raked, (II. iv, 86–7)

or,

> the quick forge and working-house of thought, (V Chor. 23).

Other images, like those of the tiger, cannon, and rock, in Henry's speech before Harfleur (III. i) not only are persuasive but they create a dramatic situation of tension broken by the discharge of cannon that concludes the speech. Others again are purely descriptive, such as that remarkable piece of detailed description of the English horsemen and horses in IV. ii, 45–50.

Some more elaborate and formal devices, arising from the rigorous Elizabethan schooling in rhetoric occur. Canterbury's analogy of the kingdom of the bees demonstrates the divine ordering of the kingdom of England. The analogy was well-known, but was regarded not as a cliché but as an impressive corroboration. He uses it to stress two themes, order and obedience, and arranges his material in groups of four according to rhetorical prescription: king, magistrates, merchants, soldiers; masons, citizens, porters, justices. The inference he draws condensed in four similes is most striking not only in the general aptness of the similes but in the association of each of them with one of the four elements of which all things were composed, air, earth, water, fire (sun). Canterbury is an able rhetorician. His account of Henry's conversion employs a sequence of images and allusions linked by elegant transitions.

Ely's image of the strawberry is apt enough in the mouth of one whose strawberry beds in Holborn were famous, and apt too in view of the belief and practice of gardeners, but its emblem significance illuminates its insight. The strawberry from medieval times, noted for remaining untainted by neighbouring plants, was the symbol of purity, the man dedicated in faith, and also the fruits of the spirit.

Fluellen makes an attempt at a formal comparison, the parallel lives of Alexander and Henry V. The method was an approved one, but Fluellen following the prescribed order: birthplaces, localities, parallel incidents, honours, etc. soon finds himself in difficulties. The dramatic point of his comparison apart from lightening the mood is the establishment of both similarities and differences between the two to Henry's advantage of self-control for while Henry may give orders for the slaughter of prisoners by military necessity he does not murder his friends.

Adverse criticism has been directed at two images, Canterbury's comparison, 'her chronicle as rich with praise As is the ooze and bottom of the sea With sunken wreck and sumless treasuries' (I. ii, 163–5) has been condemned for 'ooze and bottom'. The sea, however, in Shakespeare is commonly regarded as a treasure-house particularly of jewels, and its wealth was inexhaustible. Henry's retort to Montjoy (IV. iii, 99–107) has been regarded as unsavoury and strained. But the sun was associated with honours and also with infectious vapours, and thus Henry neatly caps Montjoy's 'bodies Must lie and fester'.

Images lacking decorum and indicating disorder are placed in the mouths of the French nobles. The French King urges his nobles to rush on Henry 'as doth the melted snow Upon the valleys, whose low vassal seat The Alps doth spit and void his rheum upon' (III. v, 50–2). This was a textbook example of a harsh, indecorous image, and might well have been known to the audience. It reflects on the speaker and not on Henry. The Dauphin likens his horse to the mythical horse Pegasus, rhetorically it was a false comparison to liken a horse to a horse, just as in an absurd form Fluellen likens his fingers to his fingers (IV.

vii, 25). Again the Dauphin equates his horse with his mistress, a frivolous extravagance that leads to the ribaldry of his companions.

Shakespeare makes extensive use of proverbs in this play. Some are cited openly as a justification for a course of action, some emphasize a topic or point of view, some he modifies or even inverts, and some, subsequently proverbs, he has invented after the manner of the 'sententiae' of the schoolroom. One proverb 'No honey without gall' has been modified (II. ii, 30) so that in its context it is ironically sinister.

Henry develops a thought through a sequence of five proverbs reaching the paradox of drawing 'honey from the weed' and a 'moral from the devil' as a means of heartening himself and his brothers. Pistol offers some material advice in proverb form to his wife as he leaves for France (II. iii, 43–8). The Boy uses them to define more closely the characters of Pistol and Nym (III. ii, 30–5). In contrast with Henry the Dauphin, Orleans and the Constable proclaim their personal animosities in proverb-capping slanders (III. vii, 65–9, 104–15).

An effort of imagination is required if we are to appreciate the importance and value of the puns that Shakespeare uses so frequently. What has been regarded in recent times as the lowest form of wit, was, as Kellett has shown, used with telling force by Isaiah and St Paul and by the Greek dramatists. Among the Elizabethans it was an accepted means of showing intellectual brilliance and verbal dexterity. Shakespeare enlarges its scope; it may produce a simple jest or emphasize a point (Lady Macbeth's

> I'll gild the faces of the grooms withall
> For it must seem their guilt

is horrifyingly emphatic, it is not hysterical).

It may sharpen the irony of an aside ('A little more than kin and less than kind'); it may be a flash of bitter insight (in *Romeo and Juliet*, the gay Mercutio mortally wounded says, 'Ask for me tomorrow, and you shall find me a grave man'); and it may be employed in an exchange of witticisms.

Sometimes Shakespeare used the two meanings of a word simultaneously, sometimes the word is repeated bearing a second meaning, or sometimes a word may have the meaning of a word of similar sound imposed upon it (in *Love's Labour's Lost* 'haud credo' is confused with 'ow'd grey doe', and in *As You Like It* 'goats' with 'Goths').

In *Henry V* the Prologue hints at twofold meanings in the invocation to 'fire', 'heaven', 'invention' and proclaims the actors' humility with a direct pun on 'ciphers' (l. 17). Henry's retort to the Dauphin's gift of tennis balls is couched in puns on 'courts', 'hazard', 'chase', 'crown', a clear demonstration of Henry's command of himself and the situation (I. ii, 263–6). The double meaning of 'hollow bosoms' (II Chor. 21) combines the ideas of both treachery and gold, a combination repeated a few lines later in 'gilt' and 'guilt' (l. 26). The Chorus, however, ends on a different note making a 'gentle pass' at the audience to avoid offending 'one stomach'. The feather-brained, garrulous Hostess among her misunderstandings inadvertently commits the magnificent pun on rheumatic (Rome-atic) (II. iii, 33). The Boy in three puns on 'boy', 'man'; 'pocket'; 'stomach', 'cast up' neatly distances himself from the cowardice and dishonesty of the 'irregular humorists' (III. ii, 25–48). The French nobles do not pun, presumably their wit is inadequate, until their squabbling leads to some sustained immature quibbling on 'mistress', 'bears', 'bridled', 'horsemanship', 'jade' (III. vii, 40–55).

Henry rounds off his debate with the three soldiers with an enforced cheerful pun on 'crowns' and clipper (IV. i, 209–10). In his wooing of Kate his overflowing high spirits express themselves in quibbles on 'like me' and 'broken music'.

KING HENRY V

CHARACTERS

KING HENRY THE FIFTH
DUKE OF GLOUCESTER ⎱ brothers to the King
DUKE OF BEDFORD ⎰
DUKE OF EXETER, uncle to the King
DUKE OF YORK, cousin to the King
EARLS OF SALISBURY, WESTMORELAND, and WARWICK
ARCHBISHOP OF CANTERBURY
BISHOP OF ELY
EARL OF CAMBRIDGE
LORD SCROOP
SIR THOMAS GRAY
SIR THOMAS ERPINGHAM, GOWER, FLUELLEN, MACMORRIS,
JAMY, officers in King Henry's army
BATES, COURT, WILLIAMS, soldiers in the same
PISTOL, NYM, BARDOLPH
Boy
A Herald
CHARLES THE SIXTH, King of France
LEWIS, the Dauphin
DUKES OF BURGUNDY, ORLEANS, BERRI, BRETAGNE, and
BOURBON
The CONSTABLE of France
RAMBURES and GRANDPRÉ, French Lords
Governor of Harfleur
MONTJOY, a French Herald
Ambassadors to the King of England

ISABEL, Queen of France
KATHARINE, daughter to Charles and Isabel

Characters

ALICE, a lady attending on her
Hostess of a tavern in Eastcheap, formerly Mistress Quickly, and now married to Pistol

Lords, Ladies, Officers, Soldiers, Citizens, Messengers, and Attendants

Chorus

SCENE: *England; afterwards France*

S.D.   *Enter Prologue.* The actor speaking the prologue usually appeared in a long black velvet coat, occasionally as suited to the theme of war he appeared in arms, as in *Troilus and Cressida.* Which is more apt here?

Any preliminary fanfare? A dignified, impressive entry is required. Should his speaking be—formal, declamatory, intimate, chatty, conversational, resonant, emotional, grave, urgent?

1–2   *O ... invention.* An appeal to the muse for inspiration was the traditional beginning of an epic poem. This is the only prologue in Shakespeare's plays that has such an invocation.

1   *muse,* a goddess patron of one of the arts. *fire.* The lightest of the four elements (earth, air, fire, water) of which the universe was supposed to be made. It naturally ascended to the highest sphere of the heavens which were accordingly the brightest. Poetic inspiration was held to be of heavenly source, and of fiery quality; fire, as here was also an attribute and symbol of war.

2   *brightest ... invention,* the sublime and divine source of poetic inspiration. *invention,* (*a*) a work of imagination, (*b*) a rhetorical term for the discovery of topics.

3–6   *A ... Mars.* The traditional subject matter of epic poems was war, the characters were kings and princes.

4   *swelling,* magnificent, uplifting, impressive, exalting.

5   *like himself,* (*a*) incomparable, unique, (*b*) in his true likeness.

6   *port,* bearing, mighty style. *Mars.* The Roman god of war.

7   *Leashed,* i.e. three together.

8   *Crouch,* i.e. ready to spring. *But ... all.* Any change in tone, or style? *gentles all,* a flattering gentling their condition in contrast with the 'flat unraised spirits'.

9   *flat unraised spirits,* dull uninspired players.

10   *scaffold,* stage.

11   *object,* spectacle, theme. *cockpit,* i.e. tiny circle.

13   *O.* Possibly a reference to the Curtain theatre. The Globe theatre was not completed until after the composition of the play. *the very casques,* even the casques (helmets), much less the men.

14   *affright the air.* Air was thought to receive impressions from events. See *Troilus and Cressida,* IV. v, 4.

15   *O, pardon, since,* i.e. pardon me for mentioning this 'O', but ... *crooked figure,* nought.

16   *Attest ... million,* may in its humble unit position increase the total value of the number to a million.

Enter Prologue

O for a muse of fire, that would ascend
The brightest heaven of invention;
A kingdom for a stage, princes to act,
And monarchs to behold the swelling scene.
Then should the warlike Harry, like himself,
Assume the port of Mars, and at his heels,
Leashed in like hounds, should famine, sword, and fire
Crouch for employment. But pardon, gentles all,
The flat unraised spirits that hath dared
On this unworthy scaffold to bring forth   10
So great an object. Can this cockpit hold
The vasty fields of France? Or may we cram
Within this wooden O the very casques
That did affright the air at Agincourt?
O, pardon, since a crooked figure may
Attest in little place a million;

17   *ciphers*, mere nothings. *account*, (*a*) sum total, (*b*) story (Dover
      Wilson).

18   *On . . . work*, stimulate your powers of imagination.

21   *abutting*, bordering, facing.

22   *perilous narrow ocean*. The English Channel notorious for ship-
      wrecks.

23–4 *Piece . . . man*, i.e. Use your imagination not only to fill in the
      pieces we have omitted but also by contrast to split into pieces
      what we represent by one actor.

25   *puissance*, army, forces.

27   *proud*, spirited.

28   *deck*, clothe, equip.

29   *them*, thoughts. In view of V Chor. 8–9 'them' could also refer
      to 'kings'. Which is preferable?

30   *many years*, 1414 to 1420. The story of the play which extends
      over some six years is compressed into the time taken by its
      performance.

31   *for . . . supply*, to help you in this.

       Five other plays by Shakespeare begin with a prologue, none
      is so apologetic or urgent for the co-operation of the audience as
      this one. It is concerned with the inadequacy of the stage, theatre,
      and actors, the non-observance of the unities of time and place,
      the attitude and co-operation of the audience, appearance and
      reality.

       Is this prologue—a petition, a flourish, an apology, an invoca-
      tion, a confession of failure, an hors d'œuvre, a bill of fare, a
      pep-talk, a piece of irony, or a piece of flattery?

       It has been suggested that the prologue and choruses are so
      serious and important that Shakespeare himself spoke them. On
      the other hand it has been asserted that Shakespeare did not write
      the choruses.

And let us, ciphers to this great account,
On your imaginary forces work.
Suppose within the girdle of these walls
Are now confined two mighty monarchies,   20
Whose high upreared and abutting fronts
The perilous narrow ocean parts asunder.
Piece out our imperfections with your thoughts;
Into a thousand parts divide one man,
And make imaginary puissance;
Think, when we talk of horses, that you see them
Printing their proud hoofs i' th' receiving earth.
For 'tis your thoughts that now must deck our kings,
Carry them here and there, jumping o'er times,
Turning the accomplishment of many years   30
Into an hour-glass; for the which supply,
Admit me Chorus to this history;
Who, prologue-like, your humble patience pray,
Gently to hear, kindly to judge, our play.   [*Exit*

London. The King's palace

S.D.   The two prelates enter together in conversation. Should they wear full ceremonial robes or not? Is their speech intoned, colloquial, solemn, oratorical, or impassioned? Are they—anxious, disturbed, angry, fearful, indignant, desperate, calm?

1   *that . . . urged,* Parliament is being pressed to pass that same bill.

2   *eleventh year,* 1410.

3   *had,* would have.

4   *scambling,* unruly, disordered, rebellious.

9   *temporal lands,* lands other than those consecrated for church use.

10   *testament,* will.

15   *lazars,* lepers.

21   *what prevention,* what means are there of forestalling this?

22–69   *The . . . perfected.* Prince Hal's sudden renunciation of his old dissolute ways and the astonishing brilliance of his newly manifest reformed qualities are very important in interpreting his later actions.

     That the two prelates view Hal's change as a religious pattern of regeneration, and describe it with a wealth of religious terms and images is to be expected. Why did Shakespeare give this task to these two rather than to, say, Exeter and Warwick who in *2 Henry IV* had already praised the Prince's virtues?

22   *The . . . regard.* The word 'prevention' perhaps prompts Canterbury to think of 'preventive grace', that is, the grace given by God which precedes and inspires repentance and conversion. *fair regard,* deference or obedience to divine laws.

32

ACT ONE

SCENE ONE

Enter the ARCHBISHOP OF CANTERBURY *and the*
BISHOP OF ELY

CANTERBURY: My lord, I'll tell you: that self bill is urged,
  Which in th' eleventh year of the last king's reign
  Was like, and had indeed against us passed,
  But that the scambling and unquiet time
  Did push it out of farther question.
ELY: But how, my lord, shall we resist it now?
CANTERBURY: It must be thought on. If it pass against us,
  We lose the better half of our possession.
  For all the temporal lands, which men devout
  By testament have given to the Church,   10
  Would they strip from us; being valued thus:
  As much as would maintain, to the King's honour,
  Full fifteen earls and fifteen hundred knights,
  Six thousand and two hundred good esquires;
  And to relief of lazars and weak age
  Of indigent faint souls past corporal toil,
  A hundred almshouses right well supplied;
  And to the coffers of the King beside,
  A thousand pounds by th' year. Thus runs the bill.
ELY: This would drink deep.
CANTERBURY: 'Twould drink the cup and all.   20
ELY: But what prevention?
CANTERBURY: The King is full of grace and fair regard.
ELY: And a true lover of the holy Church.

24   *courses . . . youth*, his youthful conduct. (See *1 & 2 Henry IV*.)

25–31   *The . . . spirits*. This is based on parts of the Baptismal Service
        from the *Book of Common Prayer*: the death of the old man, the
        body of sin, the burial of the old Adam and the regeneration of
        the new man, and the things that belong to the Holy Spirit dwell
        in the new man. The parallel is apt for Baptism is concerned with
        repentance, regeneration, and the gift of the spirit.

25–7   *The . . . too*. This recalls Henry's remarks to his brothers in
        2 Henry IV, V. ii, 123–4,

> My father is gone wild into his grave,
> For in his tomb lie my affections.

26   *wildness, mortified*. See *Romans*, viii. 13 'For if ye live after the
        flesh, ye shall die: but if ye through the Spirit, do mortify the
        deeds of the body, ye shall live.'

28   *Consideration*. Here perhaps divinely inspired contemplation. The
        word was associated by St Bernard of Clairvaux with repentance
        and conversion. The image of 'angel' is appropriate to the possible
        starry derivation of 'consideration'.

28–9   *like . . . him. Genesis*, iii, 23–4.

29   *offending Adam*, (*a*) Adam who sinned in the Garden of Eden,
        (*b*) the 'old Adam', or inborn evil.

30–1   *Leaving . . . spirits*. The image of Henry's body as a paradise may
        spring from the belief in the correspondences between the heavens,
        the kingdom, and man's body. See *Richard II*, III. iv, 29–107 for an
        analogy between the kingdom and a garden. But it may also
        depend on the much elaborated imagery of the 'garden enclosed'
        (*Song of Sol*. iv, 12) sometimes identified with paradise, which
        was particularly identified with the faithful man whom Christ's
        spirit inspired to the fruit of good works.

32   *scholar*, (*a*) disciple, (*b*) learned man. The combination of scholar
        and soldier in a man was regarded as the height of excellence.

33–4   *flood . . . faults*. Perhaps suggested by the baptismal washing away
        of sins and also by Hercules' labour of cleansing of the Augean
        stables by diverting a river through them.

35   *Hydra-headed*, i.e. persistent, crowding. The Hydra was a nine-
        headed monster slain by Hercules. A new head grew each time an
        old one was cut off, but Hercules' companion prevented this by
        thrusting a burning torch into each severed neck.

35–6   *wilfulness . . . seat*. In Elizabethan terms 'erected wit' ousted the
        'infected will'.

36   *seat*, power, throne.

CANTERBURY: The courses of his youth promised it not.
  The breath no sooner left his father's body,
  But that his wildness, mortified in him,
  Seemed to die too; yea, at that very moment
  Consideration like an angel came
  And whipped th' offending Adam out of him,
  Leaving his body as a paradise,   30
  T' envelop and contain celestial spirits.
  Never was such a sudden scholar made;
  Never came reformation in a flood,
  With such a heady currance scouring faults;
  Nor never Hydra-headed wilfulness
  So soon did lose his seat, and all at once,
  As in this King.

38–47 *Hear . . . garter.* The emblems of kingship, the crown, the throne, and the oil of anointing symbolized the king's supreme military power, his political and judicial authority, and his supremacy in religion. Canterbury describes Henry's excellence in all these matters, and adds the further tribute to his eloquence and oratory.

41 *commonwealth,* public welfare, state.

44 *rendered . . . music.* The conduct of war was regarded as a kind of music.

45 *cause of policy,* issue of government, matter of statecraft.

46 *Gordian knot.* In classical story Gordius the peasant, elected king of the Phrygians, dedicated his wagon to Jupiter. Legend had it that whoever untied the knot by which the wagon was secured would rule all Asia. Alexander the Great cut the knot with his sword declaring that he thus fulfilled the legend.

48 *chartered libertine,* privileged freely to wander.

49–50 *And . . . sentences.* It was held that the actual sounds were reformed in the ear of a listener.

49 *wonder,* wonderer, i.e. the air.

50 *sweet . . . sentences,* eloquent and pleasing wisdom.

51–2 *So . . . theoric,* so that from the active and practical life Henry has led has sprung this scholarly learning.

53 *glean.* See II. iv, 137–8, 'Now he weighs time Even to the utmost grain'.

54 *courses vain,* idle pursuits.

55 *companies,* companions. *rude,* rough. *shallow,* superficial.

57 *noted,* was noticeable.

58 *retirement,* withdrawal (for meditation). *sequestration,* seclusion.

59 *open . . . popularity,* mixing with common people and frequenting their resorts.
    Warwick, *2 Henry IV.* iv, 67–78, 'noted' Henry's studies,
        'The Prince but studies his companions
          Like a strange tongue . . .'

60–2 *The . . . quality.* Elizabethan gardeners observed that the strawberry flourished in the shade, and believed that near rank plants its purity was improved.

    Ely's analogy, apt in the mouth of one whose strawberry beds were well-known, can be taken as a straightforward horticultural image, but it is most likely that it has a deeper significance.

    The strawberry's immaculate purity whatever plants it was near was the theme of many emblems. L. J. Ross (*Studies in the Renaissance*, VII), discussing the widespread use of the strawberry

ELY: We are blessed in the change.

CANTERBURY: Hear him but reason in divinity,
  And all-admiring, with an inward wish
  You would desire the King were made a prelate.   40
  Hear him debate of commonwealth affairs,
  You would say it hath been all in all his study.
  List his discourse of war, and you shall hear
  A fearful battle rendered you in music.
  Turn him to any cause of policy,
  The Gordian knot of it he will unloose,
  Familiar as his garter; that when he speaks,
  The air, a chartered libertine, is still,
  And the mute wonder lurketh in men's ears,
  To steal his sweet and honeyed sentences;   50
  So that the art and practic part of life
  Must be the mistress to this theoric;
  Which is a wonder how his grace should glean it,
  Since his addiction was to courses vain,
  His companies unlettered, rude, and shallow,
  His hours filled up with riots, banquets, sports;
  And never noted in him any study,
  Any retirement, any sequestration
  From open haunts and popularity.

ELY: The strawberry grows underneath the nettle,   60
  And wholesome berries thrive and ripen best,
  Neighboured by fruit of baser quality.

37

symbol, notes that the strawberry was associated with the Virgin Mary and with Christ, and in a faithful individual it 'signified the state of grace, the possession of the image of God, or the fruit of the Spirit'.

65 *Grew . . . night.* A well-known belief of the period.

66 *yet . . . faculty*, although ability to grow is its natural function.

67 *miracles are ceased.* The Protestants held that miracles ceased after Christ.

68–9 *admit . . . perfected*, i.e. the divine grace conferred on the faithful man by which he is sanctified, i.e. the 'means of grace' in the prayer of General Thanksgiving. In Lancelot Andrews' words 'Grace does not abolish nature but perfects it'.

72 *indifferent*, impartial, unbiased.

74 *exhibiters*, introducers of a bill in Parliament.

75–81 *For . . . withal.* Is this a bribe, something that preceded the presenting of the bill, or a normal procedure following a meeting of convocation? Or is Shakespeare 'sitting on the fence'?

78 *opened*, given a brief account. *at large*, in general terms.

85 *fain*, gladly.

86 *severals*, details. *unhidden passages*, clear descent.

88 *seat*, throne.

Is Henry's reformation—Machiavellian, cynical, astute, pious, profound, superficial, spiritual, real?

See Introduction, pp. 4–10.

To what end are directed the numerous words and phrases with religious connotation: grace, mortified, consideration, paradise, celestial spirits, reformation, blessed, divinity, prelate, sequestration, contemplation, miracles, means . . . perfected?

Why is the bill referred to: it has no direct bearing on the war with France—to show up the corrupt priests, to introduce and establish Henry's piety and support for the Church, to show that Henry was not above taking a bribe, because it was in Shakespeare's source? Which of these is continued through the play?

And so the Prince obscured his contemplation
Under the veil of wildness; which, no doubt,
Grew like the summer grass, fastest by night,
Unseen, yet crescive in his faculty.

CANTERBURY: It must be so; for miracles are ceased;
And therefore we must needs admit the means
How things are perfected.

ELY: But my good lord,
How now for mitigation of this bill   70
Urged by the commons? Doth his majesty
Incline to it, or no?

CANTERBURY: He seems indifferent,
Or rather swaying more upon our part
Than cherishing th' exhibiters against us;
For I have made an offer to his majesty,
Upon our spiritual convocation,
And in regard of causes now in hand,
Which I have opened to his grace at large,
As touching France, to give a greater sum
Then ever at one time the clergy yet   80
Did to his predecessors part withal.

ELY: How did this offer seem received, my lord?

CANTERBURY: With good acceptance of his majesty;
Save that there was not time enough to hear,
As I perceived his grace would fain have done,
The severals and unhidden passages
Of his true titles to some certain dukedoms,
And generally to the crown and seat of France,
Derived from Edward, his great-grandfather.

ELY: What was th' impediment that broke this off?   90

CANTERBURY: The French ambassador upon that instant
Craved audience; and the hour I think is come
To give him hearing. Is it four o'clock?

ELY: It is.

The palace

S.D.   A ceremonial entry. Should the attendants or the King enter first? Any properties required—throne, table, stools, dais, scrolls, banners? Why is a fresh scene necessary? Clarence has no speaking part and does not appear elsewhere in the play. Should the king's brothers Gloucester, Bedford, and Clarence, be given some degree of precedence in the stage grouping?

1   *my gracious lord*. A formal title not a personal qualification.

2   *in presence*, in formal attendance on the King. *Send . . . uncle.* What stage business is required?

7–8   *God . . . it.* Any gesture or movement?

10   *justly and religiously*. Henry stresses this throughout the discussion.

11   *law Salic*. The point of this 'law' is given in l. 39. Originally it had nothing to do with the right of succession to the throne. It was a folk custom which was invoked by the French nobles to prevent a woman from ruling, and to bar the claims of Edward III through his mother.

12   *Or . . . claim.* Henry states the basis of the matter impartially.

13–17   *And . . . truth.* Henry again emphasizes the need for care and integrity in the strongest terms.

14   *fashion . . . reading*, adapt, distort, or pervert your interpretation.

15–17   *Or . . . truth*, or wickedly abuse your reasoning faculty by putting forward titles that are illegitimate and which in justice bear no relation to the truth.

16   *miscreate*. 'create' is the proper term both for legally establishing anything and for investing anyone with a title.

16–17   *right . . . colours*. The 'colour of a title' was the apparent right to it.

18–28   *For . . . mortality*. See Williams' speech IV. i, 127–37.

CANTERBURY: Then go we in, to know his embassy;
　Which I could with a ready guess declare,
　Before the Frenchman speak a word of it.
ELY: I'll wait upon you, and I long to hear it.　　　　*[Exeunt*

SCENE TWO

Enter KING HENRY, GLOUCESTER, BEDFORD, CLARENCE,
　EXETER, WARWICK, WESTMORELAND, *and Attendants*

KING HENRY: Where is my gracious lord of Canterbury?
EXETER: Not here in presence.
KING HENRY:　　　　　　　　Send for him, good uncle.
WESTMORELAND: Shall we call in th' ambassador, my liege?
KING HENRY: Not yet, my cousin. We would be resolved
　Before we hear him, of some things of weight
　That task our thoughts, concerning us and France.

Enter the ARCHBISHOP OF CANTERBURY *and the*
BISHOP OF ELY

CANTERBURY: God and his angels guard your sacred throne
　And make you long become it.
KING HENRY:　　　　　　　Sure we thank you.
　My learned lord, we pray you to proceed,
　And justly and religiously unfold　　　　　　　　10
　Why the law Salic, that they have in France,
　Or should or should not bar us in our claim.
　And God forbid, my dear and faithful lord,
　That you should fashion, wrest, or bow your reading,
　Or nicely charge your understanding soul
　With opening titles miscreate, whose right
　Suits not in native colours with the truth.
　For God doth know how many now in health

19   *approbation*, support, justification.

21   *impawn*, pledge.

27   *whose ... swords*, whose wrong-doing brings about war.

28   *waste ... mortality*, loss of all too short human lives.

29   *conjuration*, solemn oath and sacred charge.

31–2   *That ... baptism.* This echo of Canterbury's account of Henry's reformation is a kind of verification of it.

32   *sin*, original sin.

      Some see in this scene collusion between Henry and Canterbury, a hypocritical performance put on for the benefit of the nobles. Is there any sign of this in Henry's speech? How could it be indicated to the audience and not to the nobles?

33–5   *Then ... throne.* Why are the peers mentioned—to remind them of their allegiance, because they will be involved, because they are Henry's council?

37   *produce from Pharamond*, claim was established by Pharamond (a legendary king of the Salian Franks).

40   *gloze*, interpret.

49   *dishonest*, unchaste, corrupt.

Shall drop their blood in approbation
Of what your reverence shall incite us to.   20
Therefore take heed how you impawn our person,
How you awake our sleeping sword of war;
We charge you, in the name of God, take heed.
For never two such kingdoms did contend
Without much fall of blood, whose guiltless drops
Are every one a woe, a sore complaint
'Gainst him whose wrongs gives edge unto the swords,
That makes such waste in brief mortality.
Under this conjuration, speak my lord.
For we will hear, note, and believe in heart,   30
That what you speak is in your conscience washed
As pure as sin with baptism.

CANTERBURY: Then hear me gracious sovereign, and you peers,
That owe yourselves, your lives and services
To this imperial throne. There is no bar
To make against your highness' claim to France
But this, which they produce from Pharamond,
In terram Salicam mulieres ne succedant,
'No woman shall succeed in Salic land':
Which Salic land the French unjustly gloze   40
To be the realm of France, and Pharamond
The founder of this law and female bar.
Yet their own authors faithfully affirm
That the land Salic is in Germany,
Between the floods of Sala and of Elbe;
Where Charles the Great, having subdued the Saxons,
There left behind and settled certain French;
Who holding in disdain the German women,
For some dishonest manners in their life,
Established then this law; to wit, no female   50
Should be inheritrix in Salic land;
Which Salic, as I said, 'twixt Elbe and Sala,

57   *four . . . twenty.* Actually 379. See ll. 60–4.

59   *Idly,* vainly.
How do Henry and his nobles react during this disposal of the Salic Law—with gasps, murmurs of approval, laughter, nods of agreement, attentive movements or gestures?

66   *heir general,* inheritor.

72   *find,* furnish, provide. Some prefer the Quarto reading 'fine' = furbish.

74   *Conveyed . . . Lingare.* Sarcasm, i.e. he was not heir to the Lady Lingare. *Conveyed himself,* falsely made himself out to be.

82   *lineal,* in the line of descent.

Is at this day in Germany called Meissen.
Then doth it well appear, the Salic law
Was not devised for the realm of France;
Nor did the French possess the Salic land
Until four hundred one and twenty years
After defunction of King Pharamond,
Idly supposed the founder of this law,
Who died within the year of our redemption   60
Four hundred twenty-six; and Charles the Great
Subdued the Saxons, and did seat the French
Beyond the river Sala, in the year
Eight hundred five. Besides, their writers say,
King Pepin, which deposed Childeric,
Did as heir general, being descended
Of Blithild, which was daughter to King Clothair.
Make claim and title to the crown of France.
Hugh Capet also, who usurped the crown
Of Charles the duke of Lorraine, sole heir male   70
Of the true line and stock of Charles the Great,
To find his title with some shows of truth,
Though in pure truth it was corrupt and naught,
Conveyed himself as th' heir to th' Lady Lingare,
Daughter to Charlemain, who was the son
To Lewis the Emperor, and Lewis the son
Of Charles the Great. Also King Lewis the Tenth,
Who was sole heir to the usurper Capet,
Could not keep quiet in his conscience,
Wearing the crown of France, till satisfied   80
That fair Queen Isabel, his grandmother,
Was lineal of the Lady Ermengare,
Daughter to Charles the foresaid Duke of Lorraine;
By the which marriage, the line of Charles the Great
Was re-united to the crown of France.
So that, as clear as is the summer's sun,

91   *hold up.* A sarcastic echoing of 'hold', l. 89.

93-4   *And . . . titles,* and chose to attempt to cover up themselves in a
        way that hides nothing rather than to bar utterly their own illegal
        titles. Canterbury is scathing and scornful. Canterbury plays on
        'bar', ll. 12, 35, 42, 92, and now as the climax of his case reinforces
        it with 'im-', an intensive prefix, to stress its application to the
        French kings' claims.
            Some editors prefer the emendation 'embare', expose.

96   *right and conscience.* Henry asks the Archbishop to pronounce the
        justice of his claim, and whether his conscience may be clear
        according to the will of God.

99-   *When . . . daughter. Numbers,* xxvii. 8. Shakespeare follows
100   Holinshed in omitting 'and hath no son' after 'dies'.

103-4   *great-grandsire's . . . claim,* i.e. Edward III's. Henry's claim was
        through Edward's mother, Isabella, daughter of Philip IV.

107   *defeat,* Crécy, 1346.

110   *Forage in,* prey on.
111   *entertain,* engage, occupy.
112   *half.* Actually two-thirds.

114   *for,* for want of.
            Is Canterbury—bloodthirsty, emotional, nationally proud,
        pious, warlike? Any signs of rising enthusiasm in the bystanders?

119   *thrice-puissant liege.* Perhaps trebly powerful in the three things
        Henry has in common with his ancestors, ll. 116–18.

King Pepin's title, and Hugh Capet's claim,
King Lewis his satisfaction, all appear
To hold in right and title of the female;
So do the kings of France unto this day.   90
Howbeit they would hold up this Salic law
To bar your highness claiming from the female,
And rather choose to hide them in a net,
Than amply to imbar their crooked titles,
Usurped from you and your progenitors.

KING HENRY: May I with right and conscience make this
    claim?

CANTERBURY: The sin upon my head, dread sovereign.
    For in the book of Numbers is it writ,
    When the man dies, let the inheritance
    Descend unto the daughter. Gracious lord,   100
    Stand for your own, unwind your bloody flag,
    Look back into your mighty ancestors.
    Go my dread lord, to your great-grandsire's tomb,
    From whom you claim; invoke his warlike spirit,
    And your great-uncle's, Edward the Black Prince,
    Who on the French ground played a tragedy,
    Making defeat on the full power of France,
    Whiles his most mighty father on a hill
    Stood smiling to behold his lion's whelp
    Forage in blood of French nobility.   110
    O noble English, that could entertain
    With half their forces the full pride of France,
    And let another half stand laughing by,
    All out of work, and cold for action.

ELY: Awake remembrance of these valiant dead,
    And with your puissant arm renew their feats.
    You are their heir, you sit upon their throne;
    The blood and courage that renowned them
    Runs in your veins; and my thrice-puissant liege

120   *May-morn . . . youth.* Henry was 27. Youth was defined variously
from 17 to 42 or 20 to 30 years.

123   *rouse.* The technical word for a lion in pursuit of prey.

124   *lions,* princes.

128–9 *Whose . . . France,* i.e. in their enthusiasm they already imagine
themselves encamped in France.

       Why do Exeter and Westmoreland add their persuasions—out
of enthusiasm, to show that the nobles Henry's advisers, as
distinct from the royal princes, are unanimous for war, because
Henry appears unconvinced by Canterbury's oratory?

136–9 *We . . . advantages.* Henry remains unswayed by enthusiasm and
the offer of money, he is cautious and prudent. Shakespeare
significantly transfers this point from Westmoreland who raises it
in Holinshed.

       Any signs of reduced enthusiasm?

137   *lay . . . proportions,* arrange for an appropriate force.

138   *make road upon,* invade, make raids on.

139   *With all advantages,* with everything in his favour.

140   *They . . . marches,* the nobles whose duty it was to guard the
border.

143   *We . . . only.* Henry's judgment is superior to Canterbury's.
coursing snatchers, thieving hounds, swift-riding thieves. The image
is drawn from the coursing of hares by greyhounds who 'snatched'
their prey.

144   *main intendment,* overriding hostile attitude.

145   *still,* ever. *giddy,* unreliable, uncertain.

146–   *You . . . neighbourhood.* Henry also cites Edward III as a quiet
   54 factual retort to the uncritical views of that king's victories
mentioned by the others.

148   *unfurnished,* i.e. with armies, undefended.

151   *Galling,* harassing, wounding. *gleaned,* bare of defenders. *assays,*
assaults.

Is in the very May-morn of his youth, 120
Ripe for exploits and mighty enterprises.

EXETER: Your brother kings and monarchs of the earth
Do all expect that you should rouse yourself,
As did the former lions of your blood.

WESTMORELAND: They know your grace hath cause, and
means, and might;
So hath your highness. Never king of England
Had nobles richer, and more loyal subjects,
Whose hearts have left their bodies here in England,
And lie pavilioned in the fields of France.

CANTERBURY: O let their bodies follow, my dear liege, 130
With blood and sword and fire to win your right;
In aid whereof we of the spirituality
Will raise your highness such a mighty sum,
As never did the clergy at one time
Bring in to any of your ancestors.

KING HENRY: We must not only arm t' invade the French,
But lay down our proportions to defend
Against the Scot, who will make road upon us
With all advantages.

CANTERBURY: They of those marches, gracious sovereign, 140
Shall be a wall sufficient to defend
Our inland from the pilfering borderers.

KING HENRY: We do not mean the coursing snatchers only,
But fear the main intendment of the Scot,
Who hath been still a giddy neighbour to us.
For you shall read that my great-grandfather
Never went with his forces into France,
But that the Scot on his unfurnished kingdom
Came pouring like the tide into a breach,
With ample and brim fullness of his force, 150
Galling the gleaned land with hot assays,
Girding with grievous siege castles and towns;

49

154   *neighbourhood*, neighbourliness.

155   *feared*, frightened.

157   *chivalry*, noble warriors.

160   *impounded . . . stray*, put in the parish pound like a stray animal.

161   *King of Scots*, David II, captured at Nevill's Cross, 1346. According to a play *Edward III*, in which Shakespeare may have had a hand, David was taken to Edward III at Calais.
        Canterbury is contemptuous. Do his listeners respond?

163   *her.* The Folio has 'their'. Some editors prefer the Quarto reading 'your'.

164–5 *As . . . treasuries.* Pettet notes that Shakespeare's imagination was 'obsessed with the notion of the sea as a great storehouse of jewels'. Is the image decorous, inapt, irrelevant, suitable for things past?

164   *ooze and bottom*, oozy bottom.

169   *in prey*, in pursuit of her prey.

173   *tame*, pierce, cut into. A form of 'attame'. *havoc*, destroy.

175   *crushed necessity*, i.e. the need for that is the less.

177   *pretty*, good. Is the rhyme 'pretty', 'petty'—emphatic, sarcastic, neat, a balance of thought?

178–9 *armed . . . head.* The co-ordination of parts of the body corresponding with the function of the different offices in a kingdom was an established concept. See *Coriolanus*, I. i, 112–17.

180–3 *For . . . music*, though government is shared among parts differing in degree, yet all work as one in agreement, harmonizing like music to a perfect orderly conclusion.

182   *natural*, i.e. without chance happenings. *close*, (*a*) the ending of a musical theme, (*b*) unison.
        Music was frequently drawn on to illustrate harmony in the heavens, in kingdoms, and even in war. (See I. i, 44 and Introduction, p. 7.)

That England being empty of defence,
Hath shook and trembled at th' ill neighbourhood.
CANTERBURY: She hath been then more feared than harmed,
    my liege;
For hear her but exampled by herself:
When all her chivalry hath been in France,
And she a mourning widow of her nobles,
She hath herself not only well defended,
But taken and impounded as a stray   160
The King of Scots; whom she did send to France,
To fill King Edward's fame with prisoner kings,
And make her chronicle as rich with praise,
As is the ooze and bottom of the sea
With sunken wreck, and sumless treasuries.
WESTMORELAND: But there's a saying very old and true,
               'If that you will France win,
                 Then with Scotland first begin':
For once the eagle England being in prey,
To her unguarded nest the weasel Scot   170
Comes sneaking, and so sucks her princely eggs,
Playing the mouse in absence of the cat,
To tame and havoc more than she can eat.
EXETER: It follows then the cat must stay at home,
Yet that is but a crushed necessity,
Since we have locks to safeguard necessaries,
And pretty traps to catch the petty thieves.
While that the armed hand doth fight abroad,
Th' advised head defends itself at home.
For government, though high, and low, and lower,   180
Put into parts, doth keep in one consent,
Congreeing in a full and natural close,
Like music.

183-7 *Therefore . . . obedience.* The obedience of subjects to their rulers was regarded with such urgency that it was made the theme of one of the homilies appointed to be read in the churches. It was claimed to be divinely ordained.

185 *endeavour,* effort. Perhaps the word here has something of its original sense of 'duty'.

187- *for . . . drone.* A very famous comparison used by many authors
204 before Shakespeare. Perhaps Shakespeare here was influenced by Virgil's *Georgics,* IV, 152 ff. For this and the following images see Introduction, p. 22.

188 *rule in nature,* ordered provision of nature.

189 *act of order,* ordered way of life.

190 *king,* i.e. queen. *sorts,* different ranks.

191 *correct,* administer justice.

192 *venture,* risk.

194 *boot,* booty, plunder.

195-6 *Which . . . emperor.* Elizabeth's freebooters were not always so obedient.

197 *busied . . . majesty,* busily engaged in his royal duties. *surveys,* watches over, oversees.

198 *singing.* Suggestive of harmony. Perhaps 'merry march' (l. 195) and 'hum' (l. 202) hint at the same idea.

202 *sad-eyed,* with serious looks. *surly hum,* stern voice.

203 *executors pale,* death pale executioners.

204 *lazy yawning drone,* i.e. whose 'endeavour' is not 'in continual motion'.

What responses should Canterbury's listeners make to this analogy?

205-6 *having . . . consent,* being linked in all respects by a common purpose.

206 *may work contrariously,* may carry out their tasks from opposite sides, may differ in their methods.

207 *loosed several ways,* shot from different directions.

210 *dial's,* sundial's.

212 *borne,* carried out, maintained.

What purpose is served by Canterbury's description of the bees' commonwealth—virtue of obedience in a state, a reminder that obedience to a king was a law of God, that unity of purpose following obedience achieves success, that England is as well governed as the bee-hive?

CANTERBURY: Therefore doth heaven divide
 The state of man in divers functions,
 Setting endeavour in continual motion;
 To which is fixed, as an aim or butt,
 Obedience: for so work the honey-bees,
 Creatures that by a rule in nature teach
 The act of order to a peopled kingdom.
 They have a king, and officers of sorts,   190
 Where some like magistrates correct at home;
 Others like merchants venture trade abroad;
 Others, like soldiers armed in their stings,
 Make boot upon the summer's velvet buds;
 Which pillage they with merry march bring home
 To the tent-royal of their emperor;
 Who busied in his majesty surveys
 The singing masons building roofs of gold,
 The civil citizens kneading up the honey,
 The poor mechanic porters crowding in   200
 Their heavy burdens at his narrow gate,
 The sad-eyed justice, with his surly hum,
 Delivering o'er to executors pale
 The lazy yawning drone. I this infer,
 That many things, having full reference
 To one consent, may work contrariously;
 As many arrows loosed several ways
 Come to one mark; as many ways meet in one town;
 As many fresh streams meet in one salt sea;
 As many lines close in the dial's centre;   210
 So may a thousand actions once afoot,
 End in one purpose, and be all well borne
 Without defeat. Therefore to France, my liege.
 Divide your happy England into four,
 Whereof take you one quarter into France,
 And you withal shall make all Gallia shake.

219   *worried*, i.e. by the dog.
220   *policy*, statesmanship.
      Should the courtiers show—approval, relief, enthusiasm?

224   *bend . . . awe*, force it to accept our rule.

226   *empery*, sovereignty.

229   *Tombless*, i.e. without any memorial.
230   *with full mouth*, with eloquence.

232   *Turkish mute*. Some slaves in royal Turkish households had their
      tongues cut out to ensure that they did not betray their master's
      secrets.
233   *waxen*. Possibly tributes on wax tablets, or even wax effigies. Some
      prefer the Quarto reading 'paper'.
234–6 *Now . . . King*. Is Henry—welcoming, abrupt, haughty, brusque,
      pleasant, courteous, stern?
235–6 *for . . . King*. There were in fact two embassies. Shakespeare has
      made this one more offensive by its implication that the French
      king has ignored Henry's demands.

239   *sparingly . . . off*, express discreetly the general trend.
      Are the ambassadors—nervous, hesitant, sarcastic, insulting,
      sneering, frightened?

242   *Unto . . . subject*, to whose royal and divine grace my passions are
      as strictly subjected as are prisoners in jail. Fault has been found
      with this image, but it is very precise relying on a quibble—
      grace = (*a*) divine grace, (*b*) mercy, pardon that a king might grant
      to a prisoner.

If we, with thrice such powers left at home,
Cannot defend our own doors from the dog,
Let us be worried, and our nation lose
The name of hardiness and policy.   220
KING HENRY: Call in the messengers sent from the Dauphin.
                                        [*Exeunt some Attendants*
Now are we well resolved, and by God's help,
And yours, the noble sinews of our power,
France being ours, we'll bend it to our awe,
Or break it all to pieces. Or there we'll sit,
Ruling in large and ample empery
O'er France, and all her almost kingly dukedoms,
Or lay these bones in an unworthy urn,
Tombless, with no remembrance over them.
Either our history shall with full mouth   230
Speak freely of our acts, or else our grave,
Like Turkish mute, shall have a tongueless mouth,
Not worshipped with a waxen epitaph.

Enter Ambassadors of France

Now are we well prepared to know the pleasure
Of our fair cousin Dauphin; for we hear
Your greeting is from him, not from the King.
FIRST AMBASSADOR: May't please your majesty to give us
      leave
Freely to render what we have in charge;
Or shall we sparingly show you far off
The Dauphin's meaning, and our embassy?   240
KING HENRY: We are no tyrant, but a christian king:
      Unto whose grace our passion is as subject
      As is our wretches fettered in our prisons;
      Therefore with frank, and uncurbed plainness,
      Tell us the Dauphin's mind.
FIRST AMBASSADOR: Thus then in few.

247   *certain*, specified.

250   *you . . . youth*, your action smacks of youthful irresponsibility.

251   *be advised*, take care, think it over.

252   *galliard*, lively dance.

254   *meeter*, more suitable.

255   *tun*, barrel. *in lieu of*, in exchange for.

      Are the nobles—enraged, amused, unmoved? What movements or stage business are appropriate?

      Does Henry show any reaction to this insult?

259   *pleasant*, (*a*) agreeable (ironic), (*b*) merry at our expense.

260   *pains*, care. Perhaps there is some irony in the antithesis 'pleasant', 'pains', and a hint at the painful uneasiness of the ambassadors.

261–6 *When . . . chases.* Royal tennis, as distinct from the modern lawn tennis, was played in a rectangular court enclosed by walls. The two shorter opposite walls were pierced by galleries called hazards. String rackets were used to drive a leathern hair-stuffed ball over a low net. Winning points were gained when the ball was driven into the opponent's hazard, and when he failed to prevent it bouncing twice ('chase').

263   *strike . . . hazard*, (*a*) win a rally, (*b*) win the French throne. *crown*, (*a*) coin (stake money), (*b*) throne. 'The method of scoring in royal tennis is apparently derived from the practice of betting on the game in the reign of Louis X, 1289–1316. The normal stake was a "couronne" (crown) or "paume" worth 60 sous (Florio, *Second Frutes*, 1591, pp. 25–7). Each scoring point was calculated as a denier d'or (15 sous) until the first player to reach 60 sous won the final point which was called "couronne" ' (Arden).

264   *wrangler*, (*a*) opponent, (*b*) disputant in academic exercises.

265   *courts*, (*a*) law courts, (*b*) tennis courts, (*c*) royal courts. *France*, (*a*) the country, (*b*) a tennis court. (See Dekker, *Gull's Horn-book*, ed. 1905, p. 51.)

266   *chases*, (*a*) legal cases over claims to the throne, (*b*) points in tennis, (*c*) warlike hunting.

      With what has Henry handled the situation—composure, anger, control, brilliant verbal victory, feeble punning, intellectual mastery, wit, scathing sarcasm, boasting, justifiable retorts, good humour, tennis-like return of the jest?

      Do Henry's nobles—laugh, applaud, whisper, remain silent and still?

267   *comes o'er us*, taunts us with, throws in our face.

268   *Not . . . them.* See notes to I. i, 51–2, 66.

Your highness lately sending into France,
Did claim some certain dukedoms, in the right
Of your great predecessor, King Edward the Third.
In answer of which claim, the Prince our master
Says that you savour too much of your youth, 250
And bids you be advised. There's nought in France,
That can be with a nimble galliard won;
You cannot revel into dukedoms there.
He therefore sends you, meeter for your spirit,
This tun of treasure; and in lieu of this,
Desires you let the dukedoms that you claim
Hear no more of you. This the Dauphin speaks.
KING HENRY: What treasure uncle?
EXETER: Tennis-balls, my liege.
KING HENRY: We are glad the Dauphin is so pleasant with us.
His present and your pains we thank you for. 260
When we have matched our rackets to these balls,
We will in France, by God's grace, play a set
Shall strike his father's crown into the hazard.
Tell him he hath made a match with such a wrangler,
That all the courts of France will be disturbed
With chases. And we understand him well,
How he comes o'er us with our wilder days,
Not measuring what use we made of them.

269– *We . . . home.* Ironical, i.e. that is what the Dauphin assumed.
72

269   *seat*, throne.

271   *'tis ever common*, it is common knowledge.

273   *state*, (*a*) royal presence, (*b*) throne.

274   *sail of greatness.* See Sonnet 86 for a similar image. 'Was it the proud full sail of his great verse.'

275   *rouse me*, (*a*) ascend (to my throne), (*b*) come forth like a lion.

278– *rise . . . us*, i.e. like the sun the image of royalty.
80

282–8 *and . . . scorn.* It is significant that the blame is placed on the Dauphin's frivolity and irresponsibility.

287–8 Is the rhyme significant or not?

289– *But . . . cause.* Henry's piety and his insistence that he is carrying
93   out the will of God in making war with France are stressed throughout the play. See Introduction, pp. 5–9.

295   *savour . . . wit.* 'Savour' perhaps marks a retort for l. 250.

299   *blush.* With shame or anger?

300   *happy hour*, favourable moment.

We never valued this poor seat of England,
And therefore, living hence, did give ourself   270
To barbarous licence; as 'tis ever common,
That men are merriest when they are from home.
But tell the Dauphin, I will keep my state,
Be like a king, and show my sail of greatness
When I do rouse me in my throne of France.
For that I have laid by my majesty,
And plodded like a man for working-days.
But I will rise there with so full a glory,
That I will dazzle all the eyes of France,
Yea, strike the Dauphin blind to look on us.   280
And tell the pleasant Prince this mock of his
Hath turned his balls to gun-stones, and his soul
Shall stand sore charged for the wasteful vengeance
That shall fly with them; for many a thousand widows
Shall this his mock mock out of their dear husbands;
Mock mothers from their sons, mock castles down;
And some are yet ungotten and unborn,
That shall have cause to curse the Dauphin's scorn.
But this lies all within the will of God,
To whom I do appeal, and in whose name   290
Tell you the Dauphin, I am coming on,
To venge me as I may, and to put forth
My rightful hand in a well-hallowed cause.
So get you hence in peace; and tell the Dauphin,
His jest will savour but of shallow wit,
When thousands weep more than did laugh at it.
Convey them with safe conduct. Fare you well.

                            [Exeunt Ambassadors

EXETER: This was a merry message.
KING HENRY: We hope to make the sender blush at it.
Therefore, my lords, omit no happy hour   300
That may give furtherance to our expedition.

303   *Save . . . business.* Prayers that precede action.

310   *fair action*, honourable expedition.

s.d.   The scene ends with a ceremonial departure.

   Is Henry—hypocritical, sincere, sarcastic, vengeful, dignified, irascible, priggish, humorous, quick-witted, bullying, determined, prudent, blackmailing?

   The concentration of the French attitude in the tennis balls incident is an effective dramatic conclusion to the scene. Shakespeare significantly follows Hall in placing the incident here, and not Holinshed who places it before the meeting of Parliament.

For we have now no thought in us but France,
Save those to God, that run before our business.
Therefore let our proportions for these wars
Be soon collected, and all things thought upon
That may with reasonable swiftness add
More feathers to our wings; for God before,
We'll chide this Dauphin at his father's door.
Therefore let every man now task his thought,
That this fair action may on foot be brought.   310
                                                              [*Exeunt*

Chorus

s.d.   Does the Chorus break the dramatic illusion or enhance the play as a spectacle, or tightly link the dramatic action?

1   *Now . . . fire.* See Prologue 1.

2   *silken . . . lies,* the soft luxuries of courtly leisure are set aside.

6   *mirror,* pattern of perfection.

7   *with winged heels,* speedily. *Mercuries.* In classical myth Mercury was the messenger and herald of the gods. He wore winged sandals and cap, and carried a winged rod.

9–10   *And . . . coronets,* i.e. the promise of victories and conquests. A sword ringed by crowns was a device of Edward III, 'either in allusion to the three great victories of his reign—Crécy, Neville's Cross, and Poictiers—or to the kingdoms of England, France, and of the Romans, the latter crown having been offered to him by the Electors' (Scott-Giles, *Shakespeare's Heraldry*).

9   *hilts,* the cross guard.

12   *intelligence,* knowledge, espionage.

13   *dreadful,* fear inspiring.

14   *pale policy,* frightened plotting, or deadly intrigue, treacherous conspiracy.

16   *model . . . greatness,* small replica of the greatness that is within you.

17   *Like . . . heart.* It was proverbial that greatness of soul or heart was often found in a small body.

18   *would,* would have.

19   *kind and natural,* filial and true in their nature.

21   *A . . . bosoms,* i.e. by contrast with England's 'inward greatness' and 'mighty heart'. *nest,* i.e. of vipers. *hollow,* (*a*) empty, (*b*) false. *bosoms,* (*a*) hearts, (*b*) receptacle for money in the bosom of a dress.

22   *treacherous,* as payment to traitors.

26   *gilt,* gold. *guilt.* The pun is common in Shakespeare, see *Macbeth,* II. ii, 56–7, but it is not facetious, it is emphatic.

27   *Confirmed conspiracy,* agreed to conspire.

ACT TWO

Flourish. Enter Chorus

CHORUS: Now all the youth of England are on fire,
And silken dalliance in the wardrobe lies.
Now thrive the armourers, and honour's thought
Reigns solely in the breast of every man.
They sell the pasture now to buy the horse,
Following the mirror of all christian kings,
With winged heels, as English Mercuries.
For now sits expectation in the air,
And hides a sword from hilts unto the point
With crowns imperial, crowns and coronets,   10
Promised to Harry and his followers.
The French advised by good intelligence
Of this most dreadful preparation,
Shake in their fear, and with pale policy
Seek to divert the English purposes.
O England—model to thy inward greatness,
Like little body with a mighty heart—
What mightst thou do, that honour would thee do,
Were all thy children kind and natural.
But see, thy fault France hath in thee found out,   20
A nest of hollow bosoms, which he fills
With treacherous crowns; and three corrupted men,
One, Richard Earl of Cambridge, and the second,
Henry Lord Scroop of Masham, and the third,
Sir Thomas Gray knight, of Northumberland,
Have for the gilt of France—O guilt indeed—
Confirmed conspiracy with fearful France;

63

28   *grace of kings*, i.e. divinely graced. See Introduction, p. 9.

29   *hell and treason*, i.e. hellish treason. *hell*. In opposition to 'grace'.

31   *digest*, (*a*) put in proper order, (*b*) assimilate.

32   *abuse*, i.e. the breaking of the dramatic unity of place. *force a play*, (*a*) compel, force through, (*b*) stuff, spice; i.e. prepare by seasoning or stuffing and following the image in digest (l. 31), and perhaps reflected by 'stomach' (l. 40).

40   *offend one stomach*, (*a*) displease any taste, (*b*) upset any digestion with sea-sickness.

41–2   *But . . . scene*. See Preface 1–2.

    A strained wooing of the audience's approval has been noted in ll. 31–40.

London: in front of the Boar's Head tavern

S.D.   Should the entry be in military fashion, or swaggeringly or furtively? Is there any indication of character in their methods of entry? See the Boy's comments in III. ii, 25–47.

    It has been suggested that Nym is short in stature. How should he be dressed—in tatters, mixed garments, over-large hose, extravagant headgear, with a very large or very small sword? He is apparently 'marvellous hairy (leonine, see note to l. 48), about the face'. Should his voice be squeaky, husky, surly, high-pitched, harsh, cockney, strained, slow, impedimented, rapid, stuttering?

    Bardolph is fiery faced, blustering, cowardly although not so vociferous as Pistol. He should have some soldierly equipment about him.

1   *Nym*. In thieves' slang a 'nym' was a thief.

2   *Lieutenant Bardolph*. Promoted since *2 Henry IV* though Nym forgets later on, III. ii, 2.

3   *Ancient*, ensign, standard-bearer. Ironically a post demanding great courage.

4–5   *but . . . smiles*, but when the right time comes I shall greet him with smiles.

6   *wink . . . iron*, shut my eyes and stick out my sword.

6–7   *It . . . one*. Nym produces a comical stage sword.

9   *bestow a breakfast*, treat you to a breakfast. Bardolph speaks grandly, but breakfast was a slight and hardly convivial meal.

10   *sworn brothers*, brotherhood or gang of thieves.

And by their hands this grace of kings must die,
If hell and treason hold their promises,
Ere he take ship for France, and in Southampton.   30
Linger your patience on, and we'll digest
Th' abuse of distance; force a play.
The sum is paid, the traitors are agreed,
The King is set from London, and the scene
Is now transported, gentles, to Southampton;
There is the playhouse now, there must you sit,
And thence to France shall we convey you safe,
And bring you back, charming the narrow seas
To give you gentle pass; for if we may,
We'll not offend one stomach with our play.   40
But till the King come forth, and not till then,
Unto Southampton do we shift our scene.   [*Exit*

SCENE ONE

Enter CORPORAL NYM *and* LIEUTENANT BARDOLPH

BARDOLPH: Well met Corporal Nym.

NYM: Good morrow Lieutenant Bardolph.

BARDOLPH: What, are Ancient Pistol and you friends yet?

NYM: For my part, I care not. I say little; but when time shall
serve, there shall be smiles, but that shall be as it may. I dare
not fight, but I will wink and hold out mine iron. It is a simple
one, but what though? It will toast cheese, and it will endure
cold as another man's sword will; and there's an end.   8

BARDOLPH: I will bestow a breakfast to make you friends; and
we'll be all three sworn brothers to France. Let it be so, good
Corporal Nym.

NYM: Faith, I will live so long as I may, that's the certain of it;

King Henry V

14   *rest*, last throw. A term from the game of primero. *rendezvous of it*, where it all ends, i.e. in France. Nym airs his French.

17   *troth-plight*, betrothed. A binding contract.
18–20 *Men . . . edges*. Nym mutters dark hints of a cowardly revenge.

21   *Though . . . plod*, patience is wearisome but it succeeds in the end.
S.D.   An entry suitable to their newly married state is required. Is Pistol tall, short, stout, bearded, etc., flamboyantly dressed, loud-mouthed, swaggering, mincing, effeminate?

24   *be patient here*. Stressed to remind Nym of his belief in patience (l. 22). Is Nym showing impatience or not? *How . . . Pistol*. Some following the Quarto give this speech to Nym. In that case 'mine host' should be emphasized sarcastically, i.e. Pistol is no longer a soldier of rank but a mere tavern keeper.
25   *tike*, (a) mongrel, (b) low-bred twerp.

31   *Lady*, Virgin Mary. *here*. The Folio has 'hewne', the Quarto has 'O Lord heeres Corporal Nim', and some editors prefer the emendation 'drawn'.
32   *wilful . . . murder*. When excited the Hostess' vocabulary becomes erratic. See ll. 37–8.
33   *Good . . . here*. Any action?
34   *Pish*. The very slightest defiance. How should it be uttered—faintly, firmly, flatly, fiercely? Any accompanying gesture?
35–6 *Thou . . . Iceland*, you long-haired, pointed-eared cur.
37–8 *show . . . sword*. An unusual way of showing valour.
39   *shog off*, push off. *solus*, (a) alone, (b) unmarried (Hotson).
40   *viper vile*. Pistol affects alliteration.
41–5 *The . . . bowels*. A detailed curse.

43   *maw*, stomach. *perdy*, by God.
44   *nasty*, filthy.

and when I cannot live any longer, I will do as I may. That is
my rest, that is the rendezvous of it.

BARDOLPH: It is certain corporal, that he is married to Nell
Quickly, and certainly she did you wrong, for you were
troth-plight to her.   17

NYM: I cannot tell. Things must be as they may. Men may
sleep, and they may have their throats about them at that
time; and some say knives have edges. It must be as it may.
Though patience be a tired mare, yet she will plod. There must
be conclusions. Well, I cannot tell.

Enter PISTOL *and Hostess*

BARDOLPH: Here comes Ancient Pistol and his wife. Good
corporal, be patient here. How now, mine host Pistol!

PISTOL: Base tike, call'st thou me host?
Now by this hand I swear I scorn the term;
Nor shall my Nell keep lodgers.   27

HOSTESS: No by my troth, not long. For we cannot lodge and
board a dozen or fourteen gentlewomen that live honestly by
the prick of their needles, but it will be thought we keep a
bawdy-house straight. O well a day Lady, if he be not here
now. We shall see wilful adultery and murder committed.

BARDOLPH: Good lieutenant, good corporal, offer nothing here.

NYM: Pish!

PISTOL: Pish for thee, Iceland dog! Thou prick-eared cur of
Iceland!

HOSTESS: Good Corporal Nym show thy valour, and put up
your sword.

NYM: Will you shog off? I would have you solus.

PISTOL: 'Solus,' egregious dog? O viper vile!   40
The 'solus' in thy most mervailous face;
The 'solus' in thy teeth, and in thy throat,
And in thy hateful lungs, yea in thy maw perdy,
And which is worse, within thy nasty mouth!

King Henry V

45   *I . . . bowels*, I curse you in your guts with a 'solus'.

46   *take*, (a) strike, (b) curse. *cock is up*, the trigger is set for firing, i.e. Pistol's blood is up.

48   *Barbason*. According to *Merry Wives of Windsor*, II. ii, 269–70, the name of a devil. Dover Wilson suggests that it is Marbas or Barbas, a fiend that appeared like a raging lion. *conjure*, put a spell on, curse.

48–9   *I . . . well*. I'm in the mood to give you a pretty good beating.

49–50   *If . . . rapier*, if you use foul language with me Pistol, I'll cleanse you by sticking my rapier in you.

50   *scour*. A pistol barrel was 'foul' after it was fired, and it was cleaned by pushing a scouring rod through it.

50–1   *in fair terms*. Used elsewhere for 'in words and not in deeds'. Here and in l. 61 perhaps it means 'in polite fashion'.

52   *that's . . . it*, that's the way of it.

53   *wight*, fellow, creature.

54   *doting death*. The idea that death loved its victims was common. See *Romeo and Juliet*, V. iii, 103–5.

55   *exhale*, draw.
     Pistol's speech is filled with echoes of the alliterative melodramatic romantic poems parodied by Shakespeare in the Pyramus and Thisby play in *A Midsummer Night's Dream*.

58   *An . . . abate*. Pistol's courage also 'abates'.

60   *tall*, brave, high.

63   *Couple a gorge*. Pistol's mock-French phrase is one of Nym's 'fair terms' for 'cut thy throat'.

65   *hound of Crete*. Dover Wilson refers to Golding's translation of Ovid's *Metamorphoses*, III. 267 for the words 'shaggy rug' (i.e. hound).

66   *spital*, hospital.

67   *powdering-tub of infamy*, (a) heated tub to treat venereal diseases by sweating, (b) a tub for preserving beef in salt.

68   *lazar . . . kind*, diseased whore of the Cressida variety. *kite*, (a) bird of prey, (b) one who preys on others. Perhaps a glance at 'kit' = whore. *Cressid's*. The popular medieval story of Troilus and Cressida was told in English by Chaucer, Lydgate, and Henryson. Cressida, who had accepted the love of Troilus, one of the sons of King Priam of Troy, was sent as a hostage to the Greek besiegers of that city. She immediately became the mistress of a Greek, Diomede. According to Henryson she was punished by

68

I do retort the 'solus' in thy bowels;
For I can take, and Pistol's cock is up,
And flashing fire will follow.

NYM: I am not Barbason, you cannot conjure me. I have an humour to knock you indifferently well. If you grow foul with me, Pistol, I will scour you with my rapier, as I may, in fair terms. If you would walk off, I would prick your guts a little in good terms, as I may; and that's the humour of it.   52

PISTOL: O braggart vile and damned furious wight.
The grave doth gape, and doting death is near.
Therefore exhale.

BARDOLPH: Hear me, hear me what I say. He that strikes the first stroke, I'll run him up to the hilts, as I am a soldier.

PISTOL: An oath of mickle might, and fury shall abate.
Give me thy fist, thy fore-foot to me give.
Thy spirits are most tall.   60

NYM: I will cut thy throat one time or other in fair terms, that is the humour of it.

PISTOL: 'Couple a gorge!'
That is the word. I thee defy again.
O hound of Crete, think'st thou my spouse to get?
No, to the spital go,
And from the powdering-tub of infamy
Fetch forth the lazar kite of Cressid's kind,

Saturn with leprosy, discarded by Diomede, and died in wretchedness in the 'Spittailhous'.

69 *Doll Tearsheet*. Falstaff's whore in *2 Henry IV*.

70-1 *I . . . she*. Pistol newly a husband echoes the marriage service: 'to have and to hold . . . forsaking all other . . .'.

70 *quondam*, former. Apart from the alliteration with Quickly is this also a quibble 'quon-dame'?

71 *pauca*, few words, in short.

s.d. The Boy enters urgent and breathless.

73 *my master*, Falstaff. *your*. Some emend to 'you'.

74-6 *Good . . . warming-pan*. For Bardolph's fiery red face see *I Henry IV*, III. iii, 20-42.

  Is the Boy—impertinent, serious, jesting?

77 *Away you rogue*. Any action?

78-9 *he'll . . . days*, that boy will end up as crow's meat on the gallows one of these days.

79 *The . . . heart*. The King (by rejecting Falstaff after the coronation, *2 Henry IV*, V. v, 48-71) has utterly disheartened him.

80 *presently*, immediately.

84 *Let . . . on*, let the seas rage with storms and fiends in hell howl for their victims, i.e. let disorder and discord remain where it is natural for them to be, and not disturb our friendship.

86 *Base . . . pays*. Perhaps Pistol's adjustment of the proverb, 'The poor man always pays'. *pays*, suffers, is subject to authority. The proverb sometimes was in the form 'base is the slave that is commanded'.

88 *compound*, settle. *Push home*, fight to the death.

91 *Sword . . . course*, to swear by one's sword is a serious oath and oaths must be kept.

  Some editors add after Bardolph's speech a line from the Quarto,

  Nym: 'I shall have my eight shillings I won of you at betting'

95 *noble*, 6s. 8d. Dover Wilson suggests that Pistol has deducted discount for cash down.

98 *I . . . Nym*, (*a*) by stealing, (*b*) in Nym's company.

99 *sutler*, supplier of provisions to the army.

Doll Tearsheet she by name, and her espouse.
I have, and I will hold the quondam Quickly   70
For the only she; and—pauca, there's enough.
Go to.

Enter the Boy

BOY: Mine host Pistol, you must come to my master, and your
hostess. He is very sick, and would to bed. Good Bardolph,
put thy face between his sheets, and do the office of a warming-
pan. Faith, he's very ill.

BARDOLPH: Away you rogue!

HOSTESS: By my troth he'll yield the crow a pudding one of
these days. The King has killed his heart. Good husband come
home presently.   80

[*Exeunt Hostess and Boy*

BARDOLPH: Come, shall I make you two friends? We must to
France together; why the devil should we keep knives to cut
one another's throats?

PISTOL: Let floods o'erswell, and fiends for food howl on.

NYM: You'll pay me the eight shillings I won of you at betting?

PISTOL: Base is the slave that pays.

NYM: That now I will have; that's the humour of it.

PISTOL: As manhood shall compound. Push home.

BARDOLPH: By this sword, he that makes the first thrust, I'll
kill him. By this sword, I will.   90

PISTOL: Sword is an oath, and oaths must have their course.

BARDOLPH: Corporal Nym, an thou wilt be friends, be friends.
An thou wilt not, why then be enemies with me too. Prithee
put up.

PISTOL: A noble shalt thou have, and present pay;
And liquor likewise will I give to thee,
And friendship shall combine, and brotherhood.
I'll live by Nym, and Nym shall live by me;
Is not this just? For I shall sutler be

100 *profits will accrue,* there will be pickings.
105 *As . . . women,* i.e. if you have any human feelings. The Hostess is
     agitated, fluttering, breathless.
106-7 *quotidian tertian.* The Hostess muddles two fevers. 'quotidian'
     which has daily symptoms, and 'tertian' where the symptoms
     occur on alternate days.
109 *run . . . on,* ill-treated, vented his ill-humour on.
110 *even,* long and short.
112 *fracted and corroborate.* Some assume that Pistol is muddled and
     contradicts himself. However his words may be his own version
     of the 'broken and contrite heart' of *Psalms li*. Another suggestion
     is that 'fracted'=humbled and 'corroborate'=receives grace.
     (See note in Arden edition.)
114 *passes . . . careers,* is subject to moods and unpredictable actions.
     careers, twisting, turning gallops.
115 *condole,* console, comfort.
s.d. Pistol and his wife lead a brisk exit.
     What dramatic purposes are served by this scene—to prepare
     for the final rejection by death of Falstaff, to introduce the
     irregular humorists, to present the theme that wars abroad prevent
     quarrels at home among the most disreputable (is this meant
     satirically or not), to demonstrate the virtue (or evil) of war in
     drawing thieves and knaves into the armies, to present dishonour-
     able motives and contorted language as a violent contrast to the
     dignified oratory and scrupulous self-searching of the previous
     scene, to provide comic relief with the sudden, repeated flaring up
     of the quarrelsome cowardly pair, to show that *all* the youth of
     England are 'on fire'?

Southampton. A council room

s.d. Do they enter together or from different directions. Are they
     secretive, indignant, critical, anxious? What properties are
     required—table, chairs, throne, papers?
3   *smooth and even,* smooth-faced and fair-seeming.
4-5 *As . . . loyalty,* i.e. instead of the 'treacherous crowns' and 'hollow
     bosoms' of II Chor. 21-2.
7   *interception.* In fact the Earl of March, on whose behalf the
     conspirators were plotting, informed Henry.
8   *the . . . bedfellow.* Scroop who was given exceptional privileges by
     Henry out of close friendship.

Unto the camp, and profits will accrue.   100
Give me thy hand.

NYM: I shall have my noble?

PISTOL: In cash most justly paid.

NYM: Well then, that's the humour of't.

Enter Hostess

HOSTESS: As ever you came of women, come in quickly to Sir
   John. Ah poor heart, he is so shaked of a burning quotidian
   tertian, that it is most lamentable to behold. Sweet men, come
   to him.

NYM: The King hath run bad humours on the knight, that's the
   even of it.   110

PISTOL: Nym, thou hast spoke the right;
   His heart is fracted and corroborate.

NYM: The King is a good King, but it must be as it may; he
   passes some humours and careers.

PISTOL: Let us condole the knight, for, lambkins, we will live.

                                                                    [*Exeunt*

SCENE TWO

Enter EXETER, BEDFORD, *and* WESTMORELAND

BEDFORD: 'Fore God, his grace is bold to trust these traitors.

EXETER: They shall be apprehended by and by.

WESTMORELAND: How smooth and even they do bear them-
   selves,
   As if allegiance in their bosoms sat
   Crowned with faith and constant loyalty.

BEDFORD: The King hath note of all that they intend,
   By interception which they dream not of.

EXETER: Nay, but the man that was his bedfellow,

9   *dulled and cloyed*, surfeited and glutted.

10   *foreign purse*. From the French.

10–11 *sell ... treachery*. The conspirators confessed that they intended to deliver Henry to the French or to murder him.

S.D. A formal ceremonial entry. Is a throne or chairs and table the better arrangement? Do Exeter, Bedford, and Westmoreland move away from the three conspirators to express their distrust and to help clarify the grouping for the audience.

14   *give ... thoughts*, give me your opinions.

17   *Doing ... act*, carrying out the action.

18   *in head*, together.

22–4 *That ... us*. Ominous and ironical. Any significant inflexion in Henry's voice?

25–31 *Never ... zeal*. Is this oily flattery, a statement of truth, self-condemnation?

25   *feared*, respected.

28   *sweet shade*, i.e. protection.

30   *steeped ... honey*. The image has ominous overtones since proverbially there was 'No honey without gall'. It hints at a deceitful sugaring over of hatred. *galls*, bitterness, poison.

33   *And ... hand*. Perhaps an echo of *Psalms cxxxvii*, and an allusion to the king's duty to dispense justice.

34   *quittance*, reward, payment. *desert*, worth.

36–8 *So ... services*. Is the alliteration—viperish, hissing, accidental, fawning?

Whom he hath dulled and cloyed with gracious favours,
That he should for a foreign purse so sell   10
His sovereign's life to death and treachery.

Trumpets sound. Enter KING HENRY, SCROOP,
CAMBRIDGE, GRAY, *and Attendants*

KING HENRY: Now sits the wind fair, and we will aboard.
My Lord of Cambridge, and my kind Lord of Masham,
And you, my gentle knight, give me your thoughts.
Think you not that the powers we bear with us
Will cut their passage through the force of France,
Doing the execution and the act
For which we have in head assembled them?
SCROOP: No doubt my liege, if each man do his best.
KING HENRY: I doubt not that, since we are well persuaded   20
We carry not a heart with us from hence
That grows not in a fair consent with ours,
Nor leave not one behind that doth not wish
Success and conquest to attend on us.
CAMBRIDGE: Never was monarch better feared and loved
Than is your majesty; there's not, I think, a subject
That sits in heart-grief and uneasiness
Under the sweet shade of your government.
GRAY: True: those that were your father's enemies
Have steeped their galls in honey and do serve you   30
With hearts create of duty and of zeal.
KING HENRY: We therefore have great cause of thankfulness,
And shall forget the office of our hand
Sooner than quittance of desert and merit
According to the weight and worthiness.
SCROOP: So service shall with steeled sinews toil,
And labour shall refresh itself with hope,
To do your grace incessant services.
KING HENRY: We judge no less. Uncle of Exeter,

40   *Enlarge*, set free.

41   *railed against*, made abusive remarks.

43   *on . . . advice*, now he is more sensible, on his thinking more
        wisely.
            How does Exeter carry out the order? Do the nobles show
        reaction to Henry's command?

44   *security*, over-confidence.

45–6   *lest . . . kind*, lest by allowing him to go free you set an example
        that encourages others to behave as he has done.
            Is Scroop sincere? Is his advice justifiable?

51   *much correction*, severe punishment.

52   *too . . . me*. Ironical weighted words.

53   *heavy orisons*, weighty prayers.

54–5   *If . . . at*. Proverbially one should turn a blind eye to little faults.

54   *proceeding on distemper*, committed while drunk.

55   *how . . . eye*, how wide shall we open our eyes, how serious a view
        shall we take.

56   *chewed . . . digested*, carefully thought out, accepted, and planned.

58–60   *Though . . . punished*. Is this—savage sarcasm, amused irony, bitter
        revenge, grief for injury? Do Henry's councillors exhibit any
        emotions?

58   *dear*, (*a*) deeply felt, (*b*) dire.

61–9   *Who . . . worthiness*. This dramatic device makes very clear to the
        audience who the conspirators are, it also increases tension and
        suspense.

61   *late*, recently appointed. Is there a quibble on 'late', former, no
        longer?

63–8   *it*, the written terms of his commission.

71–6   *Why . . . appearance*. What gestures, movements, actions are
        appropriate?

Enlarge the man committed yesterday 40
That railed against our person. We consider
It was excess of wine that set him on,
And on his more advice we pardon him.

SCROOP: That's mercy, but too much security.
Let him be punished, sovereign, lest example
Breed by his sufferance more of such a kind.

KING HENRY: O let us yet be merciful.

CAMBRIDGE: So may your highness, and yet punish too.

GRAY: Sir,
You show great mercy if you give him life, 50
After the taste of much correction.

KING HENRY: Alas, your too much love and care of me
Are heavy orisons 'gainst this poor wretch.
If little faults proceeding on distemper
Shall not be winked at, how shall we stretch our eye
When capital crimes, chewed, swallowed, and digested,
Appear before us? We'll yet enlarge that man,
Though Cambridge, Scroop, and Gray, in their dear care
And tender preservation of our person,
Would have him punished. And now to our French causes. 60
Who are the late commissioners?

CAMBRIDGE: I one my lord,
Your highness bade me ask for it today.

SCROOP: So did you me my liege.

GRAY: And I my royal sovereign.

KING HENRY: Then Richard Earl of Cambridge, there is yours;
There yours, Lord Scroop of Masham; and sir knight,
Gray of Northumberland, this same is yours.
Read them, and know I know your worthiness.
My Lord of Westmoreland, and Uncle Exeter, 70
We will aboard tonight. Why how now gentlemen?
What see you in those papers that you lose
So much complexion? Look ye how they change.

76–8   *I . . . appeal.* What action is suitable—kneeling, falling prone, clinging to Henry's knees, crawling to his feet?

79   *quick*, alive, living.

82   *For . . . bosoms*, your own arguments are directed against yourselves.

85   *English monsters.* Emphatic. *monsters*, unnatural creatures or abortions which excite wonder. Deformed creatures were naturally associated with sin.
86   *accord*, consent.
87   *appurtenants*, rights, privileges.
89   *light*, (a) clipped, (b) trivial. *lightly*, (a) falsely, (b) readily.
90   *practices*, intrigues.

92   *no . . . bounty*, to no less a degree bound by generous gifts. Is the jingle 'bounty bound' emphatic?

98–9   *That . . . use*, that might almost have turned me into a source of gold coins if you had worked upon my friendship for your financial gain. Henry plays on the theme of 'crowns' (gold) and 'practices' (ll. 89–90).
99   *use*, profit, usury, interest.
101–2   *spark . . . finger*, even a spark so tiny that it could singe only my finger.
103   *stands . . . gross*, stands out as prominently.
105–8   *Treason . . . them*, treason and murder always together, like devilish brothers vowed to assist each other, working so openly in

Their cheeks are paper. Why, what read you there,
That hath so cowarded and chased your blood
Out of appearance?

CAMBRIDGE: I do confess my fault,
And do submit me to your highness' mercy.

GRAY:
SCROOP: } To which we all appeal.

KING HENRY: The mercy that was quick in us but late
   By your own counsel is suppressed and killed.　　　　80
   You must not dare, for shame, to talk of mercy.
   For your own reasons turn into your bosoms,
   As dogs upon their masters, worrying you.
   See you, my princes, and my noble peers,
   These English monsters. My Lord of Cambridge here,
   You know how apt our love was to accord
   To furnish him with all appurtenants
   Belonging to his honour; and this man
   Hath, for a few light crowns lightly conspired
   And sworn unto the practices of France　　　　90
   To kill us here in Hampton. To the which
   This knight, no less for bounty bound to us
   Than Cambridge is, hath likewise sworn. But O,
   What shall I say to thee Lord Scroop, thou cruel,
   Ingrateful, savage, and inhuman creature?
   Thou that didst bear the key of all my counsels,
   That knew'st the very bottom of my soul,
   That almost mightst have coined me into gold,
   Wouldst thou have practised on me for thy use?
   May it be possible that foreign hire　　　　100
   Could out of thee extract one spark of evil
   That might annoy my finger? 'Tis so strange
   That, though the truth of it stands off as gross
   As black and white, my eye will scarcely see it.
   Treason and murder ever kept together,

an undertaking natural to them that it occasioned no outcry of astonishment.

109– *'gainst . . . murder*, in defiance of natural order have made the
10   association of treason and murder something to rouse astonishment.

112   *That . . . preposterously*, that succeeded in so perverting thy nature.

113   *Hath . . . voice*, is acknowledged. *voice*, vote, approval.

114   *suggest by treasons*, tempt men to commit treason.

115– *Do . . . piety*, clumsily cover over the fact of damnation with
17   patchy arguments, false analogies, and specious forms of reasoning
      tricked out with attractive shows of holiness.

116   *colours*, pretexts. A rhetorical term for proofs that are unsound.
      fetched, (*a*) derived from, (*b*) a glance at 'fetch', trick, decoy.

118   *tempered thee*, (*a*) fashioned you like wax to do his will, (*b*) tempered
      you like steel. *stand up*, (*a*) support him, (*b*) be on the attack.

120   *Unless . . . traitor*, unless to confer on you the title of Sir Traitor.
      dub. Perhaps carrying on the sword imagery implicit in 'tempered'.

121   *gulled*, deceived, duped.

122   *lion . . . world*. See *1 Pet.* v. 8 'your adversary the devil, as a
      roaring lion, walketh about, seeking whom he may devour.'

123   *Tartar*, Hell. Tartarus, in classical myth, the abode of the dead.

124   *legions*, i.e. of demons. See *Mark*, v. 9.

126   *jealousy*, suspicion.

127   *affiance*, trust.

128– *Why . . . seem*. Do these rhetorical questions show Henry's
37   detachment or his strong emotion?

132   *gross*, immoderate, excessive.

133   *not . . . blood*, not giving way to emotions.

134   *complement*, outward bearing.

136   *purged*, discriminating, selective.

137   *bolted*, sifted, refined.

139   *mark the*. The Folio has 'make thee'. *full-fraught . . . indued*, fully
      gifted and best endowed.

As two yoke-devils sworn to either's purpose,
Working so grossly in a natural cause,
That admiration did not hoop at them.
But thou, 'gainst all proportion, didst bring in
Wonder to wait on treason and on murder.   110
And whatsoever cunning fiend it was
That wrought upon thee so preposterously
Hath got the voice in hell for excellence;
All other devils that suggest by treasons
Do botch and bungle up damnation
With patches, colours, and with forms being fetched
From glistering semblances of piety.
But he that tempered thee bade thee stand up,
Gave thee no instance why thou shouldst do treason,
Unless to dub thee with the name of traitor.   120
If that same demon that hath gulled thee thus
Should with his lion gait walk the whole world,
He might return to vasty Tartar back,
And tell the legions 'I can never win
A soul so easy as that Englishman's'.
O, how hast thou with jealousy infected
The sweetness of affiance! Show men dutiful?
Why so didst thou. Seem they grave and learned?
Why so didst thou. Come they of noble family?
Why so didst thou. Seem they religious?   130
Why so didst thou. Or are they spare in diet,
Free from gross passion or of mirth or anger,
Constant in spirit, not swerving with the blood,
Garnished and decked in modest complement,
Not working with the eye without the ear,
And but in purged judgment trusting neither?
Such and so finely bolted didst thou seem.
And thus thy fall hath left a kind of blot,
To mark the full-fraught man and best indued

142 *fall*, i.e. Adam's sin. Any echo of Canterbury's thought I. i, 29? Is Henry hurt, bitter, callous, emotional, cynical, violent, enraged, extravagant?

143 *to . . . law*, to make answer to the charges.

145– *I . . . Northumberland*. Should Exeter read the charges or just
  50   announce them? Guards advance to arrest them. How are they grouped for their final speeches?

  Confessions by those about to be executed were not unusual in Shakespeare's time. The purpose here is to show that God is on Henry's side (ll. 185–6) and for the conspirators to declare their repentance in hope of salvation.

155–7 *For . . . intended*. According to Holinshed the aim of the plot was to put the Earl of March on the throne, and Cambridge hoped that he or his children would succeed March who had no children.

159 *in sufferance*, undergoing punishment.

165 *My . . . pardon*. The proverb is reversed.

166 *quit*, pardon, absolve.

169 *golden earnest*, advance payment in gold as a guarantee of payment in full after completion of the murder.

With some suspicion. I will weep for thee.   140
For this revolt of thine methinks is like
Another fall of man. Their faults are open,
Arrest them to the answer of the law;
And God acquit them of their practices.

EXETER: I arrest thee of high treason, by the name of Richard
Earl of Cambridge.

  I arrest thee of high treason, by the name of Henry Lord
Scroop of Masham.

  I arrest thee of high treason, by the name of Thomas Gray,
knight, of Northumberland.   150

SCROOP: Our purposes God justly hath discovered,
And I repent my fault more than my death,
Which I beseech your highness to forgive,
Although my body pay the price of it.

CAMBRIDGE: For me, the gold of France did not seduce,
Although I did admit it as a motive
The sooner to effect what I intended.
But God be thanked for prevention,
Which I in sufferance heartily will rejoice,
Beseeching God and you to pardon me.   160

GRAY: Never did faithful subject more rejoice
At the discovery of most dangerous treason
Than I do at this hour joy o'er myself,
Prevented from a damned enterprise.
My fault, but not my body, pardon sovereign.

KING HENRY: God quit you in his mercy. Hear your sentence.
You have conspired against our royal person,
Joined with an enemy proclaimed, and from his coffers
Received the golden earnest of our death;
Wherein you would have sold your king to slaughter,   170
His princes and his peers to servitude,
His subjects to oppression and contempt,
And his whole kingdom into desolation.

175   *tender*, preserve, care for.

181   *dear*, dire, grievous.

184   *fair*, prosperous. Henry draws comfort from the unmasking of treason not anxiety lest there should be other treachery. See Introduction, p. 7.

186   *treason . . . way*. The serpent image, a common emblem of treachery.

188   *rub*, obstacle. Particularly anything that obstructs the course of a wood in the game of bowls.

191   *in expedition*, in motion.

192   *signs . . . advance*, raise the battle flags. *signs*, ensigns, standards. A ceremonial departure.

     Shakespeare enlarges Holinshed's account of the conspiracy by adding in particular Henry's attack on Scroop and the confessions. Why does Shakespeare include this scene? The stresses in it are on God's favour in bringing the plot to light (ll. 151, 158, 185–6), and the unnatural, motiveless evil of Scroop deceived by the devil, which henceforth will throw suspicion on all virtuous men.

Outside the Boar's Head tavern

s.d.   Hostess is pleading with Pistol and clinging to him. Pistol and the others have equipment for the campaign.
     Do they march, or straggle on to the stage?
     Do they show any signs of grief?

1   *bring thee*, come with you.

3   *yearn*, mourn, grieve. Some retain the Folio reading 'earn'.

4   *vaunting veins*, boastful spirit.

5   *bristle*, rouse.

Touching our person seek we no revenge,
But we our kingdom's safety must so tender,
Whose ruin you have sought, that to her laws
We do deliver you. Get you therefore hence,
Poor miserable wretches, to your death;
The taste whereof, God of his mercy give
You patience to endure, and true repentance   180
Of all your dear offences. Bear them hence.
               [*Exeunt Cambridge, Scroop, and Gray, guarded*
Now lords, for France; the enterprise whereof
Shall be to you as us, like glorious.
We doubt not of a fair and lucky war,
Since God so graciously hath brought to light
This dangerous treason lurking in our way
To hinder our beginnings. We doubt not now
But every rub is smoothed on our way.
Then forth, dear countrymen. Let us deliver
Our puissance into the hand of God,   190
Putting it straight in expedition.
Cheerly to sea, the signs of war advance;
No king of England, if not king of France.   [*Exeunt*

SCENE THREE

Enter PISTOL, *Hostess,* NYM, BARDOLPH, *and Boy*

HOSTESS: Prithee honey-sweet husband, let me bring thee to
    Staines.
PISTOL: No; for my manly heart doth yearn.
    Bardolph, be blithe; Nym, rouse thy vaunting veins;
    Boy, bristle thy courage up; for Falstaff he is dead,
    And we must yearn therefore.

9   *Arthur's bosom.* The Hostess is thinking of Abraham's bosom in
     the story of Dives and Lazarus (*Luke*, xvi. 19–31).
10   *finer end,* i.e. than one leading to hell.
11   *an . . . child,* as innocently as a child in its baptismal robe. *a parted,*
     he died.
12–13 *ev'n . . . tide.* A common belief of the time.
13–15 *fumble . . . pen.* The Hostess's version of the famous description of
     the signs of approaching death described by Hippocrates.
15–16 *and . . . fields.* Theobald's emendation. The Folio has 'and a Table
     of greene fields'. A mass of conjecture has accumulated over this
     phrase. Misreading of 't' for 'b' and 'e' for 'd' is not unusual.
     There is a possible allusion to the 'green pastures' of *Psalms xxiii*
     in keeping with the other Biblical reference (ll. 9–10) and the
     religious tones in this speech.
18–20 *Now . . . yet,* the Hostess, good-hearted and stumbling, reverses
     the thought of 'the God of all comfort' (*2 Cor.,* i. 3).
        What does she mean to say?
24   *of,* against. *sack,* sherry.
28   *incarnate,* (*a*) in the flesh, (*b*) in red.
29   *carnation,* red.
32   *handle,* (*a*) refer to, (*b*) dally with.
33   *rheumatic,* (*a*) suffering from catarrh or a streaming cold. In
     Elizabethan terms this was an affliction of the head by too much
     of the humour phlegm which distilled its slime outwardly and
     inwardly to other parts of the body. It made 'the tongue unperfect,
     faltering and stammering . . . their words double and not intel-
     ligible, in so much that at some times they be not able to speak
     one plain word, nor in sensible terms to declare their own
     meaning'.Wine drinking, Falstaff's habit, made matters worse.Then
     they 'chatter and babble so obscurely that no man can understand
     anything of that they say.' Winny, *Frame of Order,* pp. 39–40. (*b*)
     a quibble on Rome-atic. 'room', 'Rome' and 'rheum' all had the
     same vowel sound. *whore of Babylon,* (*a*) the scarlet woman of
     Revelation, xvii. 4–5 and hence a continuation of the thought of
     'incarnate' and 'carnation', ll. 28–9. (*b*) a common abusive term
     for the Church of Rome applied particularly by the Lollards of
     whom Oldcastle (Falstaff) was one.
34–7 *Bardolph's . . . service.* See *I Henry IV,* III. iii, 20–40, 68–9.
35   *black,* sinful.
36   *fuel,* i.e. the sack that Falstaff bought for him.

BARDOLPH: Would I were with him, wheresome'er he is, either in heaven or in hell.   8

HOSTESS: Nay sure, he's not in hell; he's in Arthur's bosom, if ever man went to Arthur's bosom. A made a finer end, and went away an it had been any chrisom child; a parted ev'n just between twelve and one, ev'n at the turning o' th' tide. For after I saw him fumble with the sheets, and play with flowers, and smile upon his fingers' ends, I knew there was but one way; for his nose was as sharp as a pen, and a babbled of green fields. 'How now Sir John,' quoth I. 'What, man, be o' good cheer.' So a cried out, 'God, God, God,' three or four times. Now I, to comfort him, bid him a should not think of God; I hoped there was no need to trouble himself with any such thoughts yet. So a bade me lay more clothes on his feet. I put my hand into the bed and felt them, and they were as cold as any stone; then I felt to his knees, and so upward and upward, and all was as cold as any stone.   23

NYM: They say he cried out of sack.

HOSTESS: Ay, that a did.

BARDOLPH: And of women.

HOSTESS: Nay, that a did not.

BOY: Yes, that a did, and said they were devils incarnate.

HOSTESS: A could never abide carnation, 'twas a colour he never liked.   30

BOY: A said once the devil would have him about women.

HOSTESS: A did in some sort, indeed, handle women; but then he was rheumatic, and talked of the whore of Babylon.

BOY: Do you not remember a saw a flea stick upon Bardolph's nose, and a said it was a black soul burning in hell?

BARDOLPH: Well, the fuel is gone that maintained that fire; that's all the riches I got in his service.

NYM: Shall we shog? The King will be gone from South-ampton.

PISTOL: Come, let's away. My love, give me thy lips.   40

42   *Let senses rule*, keep your wits about you. *word*. The Folio has 'world', a variant form of 'word'. See O.E.D. world. *Pitch and pay*, cash down, spot cash.

44   *oaths are straws*. Perhaps a quibble 'oaths': 'oats'. (See *As You Like It*, III. iii, 5–6 'goats': 'Goths'; *Much Ado*, II. iii, 50–3 'noting': 'nothing'.) *men's ... wafer-cakes*, i.e. made to be broken, frail. There may be a glance at the Puritan opposition to the use of wafers at communion, i.e. that 'faith' has descended to trivialities over wafers or bread.

45   *hold-fast ... dog*. Proverbial: 'Brag is a good dog, but Holdfast is better.

46   *caveto*, take care, beware.

47   *clear thy crystals*, wipe your eyes.

48   *horse-leeches*, i.e. rapacious persons, blood-suckers.

50   *that's ... food*. The Boy deflates Pistol's extravagant speech. Blood was considered to be indigestible.

53   *I ... it*. Any gesture from the disappointed suitor?

54   *Let ... close*. Maintain good housekeeping, and keep yourself to yourself. After a final kiss they march off. What does the Hostess do—wave, weep, wail, rush off sobbing?

       What is the purpose of this scene—to give a moving account of Falstaff's death (why should Shakespeare wish to move us?), to symbolize the removal from Henry of the 'old man', the old Adam, his earlier wildness, to afford a contrast of mistrust and search for plunder to Henry's trust and rightful claim?

France: a council chamber

S.D.   A ceremonial entry. Should the nobles show—anxiety, boredom, dignity, indifference, light-heartedness?

       The grouping should allow for the reception of the embassy, l. 75.

       The French King suffered from mental illness and the Dauphin governed for him. Should he be portrayed as a sick man?

       Any properties required?

1   *Thus ... us*. Any script or other indication to support 'Thus'?

3   *To ... defences*, to see that our defences fully match their assault.

7   *line*, fortify, reinforce.

8   *means defendant*, defensive measures.

10   *gulf*, whirlpool.

Look to my chattels and my movables.
Let senses rule. The word is 'Pitch and pay':
Trust none;
For oaths are straws, men's faiths are wafer-cakes,
And hold-fast is the only dog, my duck.
Therefore caveto be thy counsellor.
Go, clear thy crystals. Yoke-fellows in arms,
Let us to France, like horse-leeches my boys,
To suck, to suck, the very blood to suck.
BOY: And that's but unwholesome food, they say.   50
PISTOL: Touch her soft mouth, and march.
BARDOLPH: Farewell hostess.   [*Kissing her*
NYM: I cannot kiss, that is the humour of it; but adieu.
PISTOL: Let housewifery appear; keep close, I thee command.
HOSTESS: Farewell; adieu.   [*Exeunt*

SCENE FOUR

Flourish. Enter the FRENCH KING, *the* DAUPHIN, *the* DUKES OF
BERRI *and* BRETAGNE, *the* CONSTABLE, *and others*

FRENCH KING: Thus comes the English with full power upon
     us,
And more than carefully it us concerns
To answer royally in our defences.
Therefore the Dukes of Berri and of Bretagne,
Of Brabant and of Orleans, shall make forth,
And you Prince Dauphin, with all swift dispatch
To line and new repair our towns of war
With men of courage, and with means defendant.
For England his approaches makes as fierce
As waters to the sucking of a gulf.   10
It fits us then to be as provident

89

12 *late examples*, i.e. Crécy, 1346, Poictiers, 1356.

13 *fatal and neglected*, fatally despised.

16 *peace . . . kingdom*. It was commonly argued that peace sapped a nation's energies.

25 *Whitsun morris-dance*. The dancers blackened their faces, hence the names, 'moorish', 'morisco', and wore bells and fancy costume. Characters from folk-stories such as Robin Hood and Maid Marian were introduced.

26 *idly kinged*, ruled by so frivolous a monarch.

27 *Her . . . borne*, her royal authority so foolishly exercised

28 *giddy, shallow, humorous*, light-headed, brainless, full of whims.

29 *That . . . not*, that her approach does not arouse any fear.

The Dauphin admits the wisdom of maintaining armed forces and defences, but he 'neglects' Henry. Should he display the characteristics he attributes to Henry? Is he—vain, sober, dignified, young, foppish, conceited? Is his speech rapid, light, slurred, lisping, high-pitched, bass?

O . . . Dauphin. The Constable and Prince Dauphin are unfriendly to each other. See III. vii.

31 *your grace*, i.e. the King.

34 *modest in exception*, restrained in raising objections.

36 forespent, previously practised.

37 *Brutus*. Lucius Junius Brutus who with others expelled the Tarquins from Rome. Previously he had feigned madness to save his life. See *Rape of Lucrece*, ll. 1807–17.

As fear may teach us out of late examples
Left by the fatal and neglected English
Upon our fields.

DAUPHIN: My most redoubted father,
It is most meet we arm us 'gainst the foe;
For peace itself should not so dull a kingdom,
Though war nor no known quarrel were in question,
But that defences, musters, preparations,
Should be maintained, assembled, and collected,
As were a war in expectation.   20
Therefore I say 'tis meet we all go forth
To view the sick and feeble parts of France;
And let us do it with no show of fear,
No, with no more than if we heard that England
Were busied with a Whitsun morris-dance.
For, my good liege, she is so idly kinged,
Her sceptre so fantastically borne
By a vain, giddy, shallow, humorous youth,
That fear attends her not.

CONSTABLE: O peace, Prince Dauphin,
You are too much mistaken in this King.   30
Question your grace the late ambassadors,
With what great state he heard their embassy,
How well supplied with noble counsellors,
How modest in exception, and withal
How terrible in constant resolution.
And you shall find his vanities forespent
Were but the outside of the Roman Brutus,
Covering discretion with a coat of folly;
As gardeners do with ordure hide those roots
That shall first spring and be most delicate.   40

DAUPHIN: Well, 'tis not so, my lord high Constable.
But though we think it so, it is no matter.
In cases of defence 'tis best to weigh

45 *so . . . filled*, so that defensive measures are fully taken.

46 *Which . . . projection*, which, if planned on a small, inadequate scale.

47 *scanting*, begrudging.

50 *fleshed upon us*, experienced in war by fighting us.

51 *bloody strain*, fierce breed.

52 *That . . . paths*, that habitually pursued us in our own lands.

54 *struck*, fought.

57 *mountain*, mighty.

61 *patterns*, excellent men.

64 *The . . . him*, his greatness and destiny to which he was born.

What point is there in the repetition of Edward III's victories. See I. ii, 100–14—to emphasize the link between Henry and the former claimant to the French throne, to stress the qualities of breed, to compare Henry's achievements with those of Edward III and the Black Prince, to introduce the epic device of declaring a pedigree?

67 *present*, immediate.

68 *chase*. An echo of Henry's 'chases', I. ii, 266.

69 *Turn head*, turn at bay (of a stag). *head*, antlers.

70 *spend their mouths*, give loudest-tongue.

The enemy more mighty than he seems;
So the proportions of defence are filled,
Which of a weak and niggardly projection
Doth like a miser spoil his coat with scanting
A little cloth.

FRENCH KING: Think we King Harry strong;
And princes, look you strongly arm to meet him.
The kindred of him hath been fleshed upon us;   50
And he is bred out of that bloody strain
That haunted us in our familiar paths.
Witness our too much memorable shame
When Cressy battle fatally was struck,
And all our princes captived by the hand
Of that black name, Edward, Black Prince of Wales;
Whiles that his mountain sire, on mountain standing
Up in the air, crowned with the golden sun,
Saw his heroical seed, and smiled to see him
Mangle the work of nature, and deface   60
The patterns that by God and by French fathers
Had twenty years been made. This is a stem
Of that victorious stock; and let us fear
The native mightiness and fate of him.

Enter a Messenger

MESSENGER: Ambassadors from Harry King of England
Do crave admittance to your majesty.

FRENCH KING: We'll give them present audience. Go, and
    bring them.   *[Exeunt Messenger and certain Lords*
You see this chase is hotly followed, friends.

DAUPHIN: Turn head, and stop pursuit; for coward dogs
Most spend their mouths when what they seem to threaten   70
Runs far before them. Good my sovereign,
Take up the English short, and let them know
Of what a monarchy you are the head,

75   *self-neglecting*, failing to stand up for yourself.

S.D.   Some formal ceremony of greeting is required. Contrast Exeter's direct approach with that of the French ambassadors, I. ii, 234–40.

78–9   *divest . . . borrowed*. For the image of the usurper in 'borrowed robes'. see *Macbeth*, V. ii, 20–2 and *The Tempest*, II. i, 263–4.

79–80   *gift . . . nations*, i.e. by divine right, by natural law arrived at by reason, and by national law and custom.

80   *'longs*, belong.

83   *ordinance of times*, traditional practice.

85   *sinister*, illegitimate. *awkward*, crooked, illegal.

86–7   *Picked . . . raked*, by grubbing among events of the remote past or sorting among long forgotten things. 'Picked' and 'raked'. The contempt is emphasized by their position.

88   *memorable line*, well-known pedigree.

89   *demonstrative*, proved.

91   *evenly*, directly, without obstacle.

94   *indirectly*, wrongfully, i.e. not by rightful descent.

95   *native*, directly descended. *challenger*, claimant.

97   *constraint*, war, violence.

100   *In . . . Jove*. Jupiter (Jove) was armed with thunderbolts.

102   *in . . . Lord*, by the mercy of God. A well-known phrase from *Phil.*, i. 8 quoted by Holinshed.

Self-love, my liege, is not so vile a sin
As self-neglecting.

Enter Lords, with EXETER *and train*

FRENCH KING: From our brother of England?
EXETER: From him, and thus he greets your majesty.
  He wills you in the name of God Almighty,
  That you divest yourself, and lay apart
  The borrowed glories that by gift of heaven,
  By law of nature and of nations, 'longs   80
  To him and to his heirs; namely the crown
  And all wide-stretched honours that pertain
  By custom and the ordinance of times
  Unto the crown of France. That you may know
  'Tis no sinister nor no awkward claim,
  Picked from the worm-holes of long-vanished days,
  Nor from the dust of old oblivion raked,
  He sends you this most memorable line,
  In every branch truly demonstrative;
  Willing you overlook this pedigree.   90
  And when you find him evenly derived
   From his most famed of famous ancestors,
  Edward the Third, he bids you then resign
  Your crown and kingdom, indirectly held
  From him the native and true challenger.
FRENCH KING: Or else what follows?
EXETER: Bloody constraint; for if you hide the crown
  Even in your hearts, there will he rake for it.
  Therefore in fierce tempest is he coming,
  In thunder and in earthquake, like a Jove,   100
  That if requiring fail, he will compel.
  And bids you in the bowels of the Lord
  Deliver up the crown, and to take mercy
  On the poor souls for whom this hungry war

106   *Turning*, placing the responsibility for.
107   *pining*. The Quarto reading, the Folio has 'privy'.
      This description of the evils of war seems to be drawn from
Hall's *Union of the Two Noble Families of Lancaster and York*.

114   *intent*, will, pleasure.

124   *womby vaultages*, hollow caverns.

126   *second accent*, echo. *ordinance*, artillery, ordnance.

129   *odds*, war.

131   *Paris balls*, an early name for tennis balls.
132   *Louvre*. The royal court in Paris. The Folio spelling 'Louer' points
a quibble with 'mistress-court'. *mistress-court*, supreme court.

137   *masters*, i.e. Henry is now in mature control. Does 'masters' hint at
a relationship with 'mistress-court', to Henry's position in France?
137-8   *Now . . . grain*, i.e. no longer a liberal distribution of wild oats.
137   *weighs time*, (a) redeems the time, (b) spends every moment
advantageously.

Opens his vasty jaws; and on your head
Turning the widows' tears, the orphans' cries,
The dead men's blood, the pining maidens' groans,
For husbands, fathers, and betrothed lovers,
That shall be swallowed in this controversy.
This is his claim, his threatening, and my message;   110
Unless the Dauphin be in presence here,
To whom expressly I bring greeting too.

FRENCH KING: For us, we will consider of this further.
Tomorrow shall you bear our full intent
Back to our brother of England.

DAUPHIN: For the Dauphin,
I stand here for him. What to him from England?

EXETER: Scorn and defiance, slight regard, contempt,
And any thing that may not misbecome
The mighty sender, doth he prize you at.
Thus says my King: an if your father's highness   120
Do not, in grant of all demands at large,
Sweeten the bitter mock you sent his majesty,
He'll call you to so hot an answer of it,
That caves and womby vaultages of France
Shall chide your trespass and return your mock
In second accent of his ordinance.

DAUPHIN: Say, if my father render fair return,
It is against my will; for I desire
Nothing but odds with England. To that end,
As matching to his youth and vanity,   130
I did present him with the Paris balls.

EXETER: He'll make your Paris Louvre shake for it,
Were it the mistress-court of mighty Europe.
And be assured, you'll find a difference,
As we his subjects have in wonder found,
Between the promise of his greener days
And these he masters now. Now he weighs time

138   *grain*, (*a*) gold weight, (*b*) smallest particle. *read*, learn.

143   *is footed*. Historically Henry landed some five months later. What is the effect of this change—to increase tension, to abridge time unobtrusively, to stress Henry's speed? (See 'hotly followed', l. 68.)

145   *breath*, breathing space.

Even to the utmost grain; that you shall read
In your own losses, if he stay in France.

FRENCH KING: Tomorrow shall you know our mind at full.

[Flourish

EXETER: Dispatch us with all speed, lest that our King   141
Come here himself to question our delay;
For he is footed in this land already.

FRENCH KING: You   shall   be   soon   dispatched   with   fair
conditions.
A night is but small breath and little pause
To answer matters of this consequence.   *[Exeunt*

Chorus

1   *imagined wing.* Again the audience is invited to use its imagination. See ll. 7, 18, 35.

4   *well-appointed*, well-equipped. *Hampton.* The Folio has 'Dover'.

5   *brave*, fine.

6   *young Phœbus*, rising sun. Phœbus Apollo in classical myth was the sun-god. *fanning*. The Folio has 'fayning'.

9   *whistle*, i.e. blown by the shipmaster.

12   *bottoms*, ships.

14   *rivage*, shore.

18   *Grapple . . . sternage*, let your thoughts cling closely to the course of this fleet. *sternage*. Probably 'stern' here has its original meaning of 'steer', and it is the course of the ship rather than the rear parts that is intended.

19   *still*, silent.

21   *pith*, strength.

24   *culled*, select. *choice-drawn*, i.e. volunteers.

27   *fatal*, deadly. *girded*, besieged.

ACT THREE

CHORUS: Thus with imagined wing our swift scene flies
   In motion of no less celerity
   Than that of thought. Suppose that you have seen
   The well-appointed King at Hampton pier
   Embark his royalty; and his brave fleet
   With silken streamers the young Phœbus fanning.
   Play with your fancies; and in them behold
   Upon the hempen tackle ship-boys climbing;
   Hear the shrill whistle which doth order give
   To sounds confused; behold the threaden sails,   10
   Borne with th' invisible and creeping wind,
   Draw the huge bottoms through the furrowed sea,
   Breasting the lofty surge. O, do but think
   You stand upon the rivage, and behold
   A city on the inconstant billows dancing.
   For so appears this fleet majestical,
   Holding due course to Harfleur. Follow, follow.
   Grapple your minds to sternage of this navy,
   And leave your England, as dead midnight still,
   Guarded with grandsires, babies, and old women,   20
   Either past or not arrived to pith and puissance.
   For who is he, whose chin is but enriched
   With one appearing hair, that will not follow
   These culled and choice-drawn cavaliers to France?
   Work, work your thoughts, and therein see a siege.
   Behold the ordnance on their carriages,
   With fatal mouths gaping on girded Harfleur.

28   *Suppose*, imagine.

32   *likes not*, is not pleasing. *nimble gunner*. Rapidity in loading and
      firing cannon was recommended practice.
33   *linstock*, a stake with a forked head to hold the gunner's slow
      match. *devilish cannon*, basilisks. See V. ii, 17.

35   *eke*. The Folio has the form 'eche', so pronounced.

Before the walls of Harfleur

S.D.   The 'alarum' is sounded on trumpets and drums, here followed
       by shouts and noises of battle. What should the soldiers do with
       the scaling-ladders? Do they enter from both sides of the stage?
       How is Henry placed to deliver his speech? Some reactions are
       necessary during the speech. See also Introduction, p. 16.

7   *conjure*, raise the spirit. The Folio has 'commune'. Editors generally
       adopt Rowe's emendation 'summon' which has little paleo-
       graphical support. See note in Arden edition.
8   *hard-favoured*, grim-faced.
9   *aspect*, appearance.
10   *portage*, portholes.
11–14 *let ... ocean*, let the frowning brow overhang the eyes as
       menacingly as a cliff juts out and hangs over its eroded foot lashed
       by the wild destructive sea.

16–17 *bend ... height*, draw up your spirit to its highest pitch. *bend up*,
       i.e. bend as a bow in archery.

Suppose the ambassador from the French comes back;
Tells Harry that the king doth offer him
Katharine his daughter, and with her to dowry,   30
Some petty and unprofitable dukedoms.
The offer likes not; and the nimble gunner
With linstock now the devilish cannon touches,
                              [*Alarum, and chambers go off*
And down goes all before them. Still be kind,
And eke out our performance with your mind.   [*Exit*

SCENE ONE

Enter KING HENRY, EXETER, BEDFORD,
GLOUCESTER
Alarum: scaling ladders at Harfleur

KING HENRY: Once more unto the breach, dear friends, once
    more;
  Or close the wall up with our English dead.
  In peace there's nothing so becomes a man
  As modest stillness and humility.
  But when the blast of war blows in our ears,
  Then imitate the action of the tiger;
  Stiffen the sinews, conjure up the blood,
  Disguise fair nature with hard-favoured rage.
  Then lend the eye a terrible aspect;
  Let it pry through the portage of the head   10
  Like the brass cannon; let the brow o'erwhelm it
  As fearfully as doth a galled rock
  O'erhang and jutty his confounded base,
  Swilled with the wild and wasteful ocean.
  Now set the teeth and stretch the nostril wide,
  Hold hard the breath, and bend up every spirit

King Henry V

17   *On ... English.* Any movement by his audiencer?
     Is this incitement bestial. relevant, inspiring, insensitive, noble?
     noblest, of most noble descent.
18   *fet*, fetched, sprung. *of war-proof*, battle-hardened.
19   *Alexanders*, i.e. Alexander the Great who lamented that there were
     no more worlds to conquer.
21   *argument*, opponents.
22   *attest*, prove.

24   *grosser blood*, inferior birth.

27   *mettle ... pasture*, fine quality of your rearing. Yeomen and
     nobles are apart on the stage so that Henry can turn from one to
     the other.
29–30 *For ... eyes*, although of humble birth you reflect in your eyes the
     spirit of the nobles.
31–2 *I ... start.* Any grouping to support this?
31   *slips*, leashes.
33   *Follow your spirit*, i.e. in spirit you are already engaged in battle.
     upon this charge, as you charge.
33, 34 *charge, George.* A rhyme.
     Should Henry lead the charge?

s.d.   Bardolph leads. Is the charge—feeble, comic, earnest, faltering?

1   *On ... breach.* Are Bardolph's words meant as a parody of
     Henry's or that Bardolph is genuinely inspired?
2   *corporal.* See II. i, 2. *knocks ... hot*, blows are too fierce.
3   *case*, set. *humour*, condition, tempo.
4   *plainsong*, a simple melody sung in unison. Here the 'simple truth'.
6–9 *Knocks ... fame.* Pistol's version of plainsong perhaps imitating
     phrases from ballads.

To his full height. On, on, you noblest English,
Whose blood is fet from fathers of war-proof;
Fathers that, like so many Alexanders,
Have in these parts from morn till even fought,   20
And sheathed their swords for lack of argument.
Dishonour not your mothers; now attest
That those whom you called fathers did beget you.
Be copy now to men of grosser blood,
And teach them how to war. And you good yeomen,
Whose limbs were made in England, show us here
The mettle of your pasture; let us swear
That you are worth your breeding, which I doubt not;
For there is none of you so mean and base
That hath not noble lustre in your eyes.   30
I see you stand like greyhounds in the slips,
Straining upon the start. The game's afoot.
Follow your spirit, and upon this charge
Cry 'God for Harry, England, and Saint George!'
                      [Exeunt. Alarum, and chambers go off

SCENE TWO

Enter NYM, BARDOLPH, PISTOL, *and Boy*

BARDOLPH: On, on, on, on, on, to the breach, to the breach!
NYM: Pray thee corporal stay, the knocks are too hot; and for
   mine own part, I have not a case of lives. The humour of it
   is too hot, that is the very plainsong of it.
PISTOL: The plainsong is most just, for humours do abound.
   Knocks go and come, God's vassals drop and die;

           And sword and shield,
           In bloody field,
           Doth win immortal fame.

13–15 *If . . . hie.* Pistol's version of the 'simple truth'.

16–17 *As . . . bough.* The Boy neatly caps Pistol's effort.
16 *truly,* (*a*) honourably, (*b*) tunefully.

s.d. A forceful entry. Fluellen in captain's accoutrements speaking with Welsh intonation.

18 *avaunt,* forward. *cullions,* scum, rogues.

19 *great duke.* This is perhaps flattery although men of noble rank did hold the rank of captains. *men of mould,* men of clay, mere mortals.
  Does Fluellen beat them, or direct them? Does Pistol cringe, kneel, fawn, run?

22 *bawcock,* fine fellow. *lenity,* mercy.

23 *These . . . humours,* i.e. 'lenity' and mercy.

25 *swashers,* swaggerers. *boy,* (*a*) servant, (*b*) boy in years (as compared with them).

27 *man,* (*a*) servant, (*b*) as much of a man as I am.

28 *antics,* freaks, oddities.

28–9 *white-livered,* cowardly, i.e. his liver the seat of courage has no blood in it.

29 *red-faced,* choleric, courageous—on the surface.

29–30 *a . . . not,* he puts a bold face on it but evades fighting.

30 *killing tongue,* i.e. kills with words only.

31 *breaks words,* (*a*) breaks promises, (*b*) quarrels.

32–3 *men . . . men.* It was proverbial that 'few words are best'.

33–4 *scorns . . . coward. Merry Wives of Windsor,* I. i, 119–20 where Nym pretends to want few words only lest a fight with Slender be delayed.

37 *purchase,* (*a*) loot, (*b*) acquiring.

41 *service.* Ironical. *carry coals,* (*a*) do the lowest of dirty jobs, (*b*) show cowardice.

BOY: Would I were in an ale-house in London! I would give all my fame for a pot of ale and safety.   11
PISTOL: And I:

>   If wishes would prevail with me,
>   My purpose should not fail with me,
>   But thither would I hie.
BOY: As duly, but not as truly,
>   As bird doth sing on bough.

Enter FLUELLEN

FLUELLEN: Up to the breach, you dogs! Avaunt, you cullions!
PISTOL: Be merciful great duke to men of mould.

>   Abate thy rage, abate thy manly rage,   20
>   Abate thy rage, great duke.

Good bawcock, bate thy rage; use lenity, sweet chuck.
NYM: These be good humours. Your honour wins bad humours.   [*Exeunt all but Boy*
BOY: As young as I am, I have observed these three swashers. I am boy to them all three, but all they three, though they would serve me, could not be man to me; for indeed three such antics do not amount to a man. For Bardolph, he is white-livered and red-faced; by the means whereof a faces it out, but fights not. For Pistol, he hath a killing tongue and a quiet sword; by the means whereof a breaks words, and keeps whole weapons. For Nym, he hath heard that men of few words are the best men, and therefore he scorns to say his prayers, lest a should be thought a coward. But his few bad words are matched with as few good deeds; for a never broke any man's head but his own, and that was against a post when he was drunk. They will steal any thing, and call it purchase. Bardolph stole a lute-case, bore it twelve leagues, and sold it for three halfpence. Nym and Bardolph are sworn brothers in filching, and in Callice they stole a fire-shovel. I knew by that piece of service the men would carry coals. They would have

42–3   *as . . . handkerchers*, as slick in and out of men's pockets as gloves or handkerchiefs.

45   *pocketing . . . wrongs*, (a) swallowing insults, (b) receiving stolen goods.

46–7   *goes . . . stomach*, (a) goes against my hardened feelings, (b) makes me sick.

47   *cast it up*, (a) give it up, (b) spew it up.
    What is the point of this soliloquy—condemnation of Falstaff's followers leading to the death of all except Pistol, contrasting picture with the standards of honour and courage of the preceding scene, comment on the display of cowardice alienating them from other soldiers, to display the Boy's wit in quibbles and antitheses?

48   *presently*, at once.

49   *mines.* The English attempted to blow holes in the city walls by mining, but the besieged prevented this.

52   *disciplines . . . war*, practice, tactics—according to treatises on the art of war.

52–3   *concavities . . . sufficient*, tunnels are inadequate.

53   *discuss*, inform, explain.

54–5   *is . . . countermines*, has himself dug countermines four yards under our mines.

63   *in his beard*, to his face.

63–4   *He . . . wars*, his orders show no more knowledge of the tactics of war.

64   *Roman disciplines.* Whether or not the military tactics and strategy of the Romans were applicable to contemporary warfare which used guns was the subject of lively controversy in the 1590's.

69   *expedition*, ready knowledge.

70   *aunchiant.* The Folio spelling and perhaps an indication of Fluellen's pronunciation.

70–1   *upon . . . directions*, as I have observed from his orders.

me as familiar with men's pockets as their gloves or their
handkerchers; which makes much against my manhood, if I
should take from another's pocket to put into mine; for it is
plain pocketing up of wrongs. I must leave them and seek
some better service. Their villainy goes against my weak
stomach, and therefore I must cast it up.   [*Exit*   47

Re-enter FLUELLEN, GOWER *following*

GOWER: Captain Fluellen, you must come presently to the
   mines; the Duke of Gloucester would speak with you.   49
FLUELLEN: To the mines? Tell you the Duke, it is not so good
   to come to the mines; for look you, the mines is not according
   to the disciplines of the war; the concavities of it is not
   sufficient; for look you, th' athversary, you may discuss unto
   the Duke, look you, is digt himself four yard under the
   countermines. By Cheshu, I think a will plow up all, if there
   is not better directions.
GOWER: The Duke of Gloucester, to whom the order of the
   siege is given, is altogether directed by an Irishman, a very
   valiant gentleman, i' faith.
FLUELLEN: It is Captain Macmorris, is it not?   60
GOWER: I think it be.
FLUELLEN: By Cheshu, he is an ass, as in the world; I will verify
   as much in his beard. He has no more directions in the true
   disciplines of the wars, look you, of the Roman disciplines, than
   is a puppy-dog.

Enter MACMORRIS *and* CAPTAIN JAMY

GOWER: Here a comes, and the Scots captain, Captain Jamy,
   with him.   67
FLUELLEN: Captain Jamy is a marvellous falorous gentleman,
   that is certain, and of great expedition and knowledge in th'
   aunchiant wars, upon my particular knowledge of his directions. By Cheshu, he will maintain his argument as well as

77   *pioners*, sappers, miners.
78–82 *By . . . done*. Is Macmorris—gentle, confused, frustrated, agitated,
      impatient, critical, flustered, sensitive, proud, tactless, impetuous?

83–9 *Captain . . . point*. There were many such discussions among
      captains which appeared in print. Barnabe Rich's *A Soldier's Wish
      to Britons Welfare* is a lengthy discussion between Captain Skill and
      Captain Pill.

91   *quit you*, join in, answer you.

101–5 *By . . . tway*. Jamy resents the suggestion that he is not doing
      anything, but he still considers that there is time for discussion.

any military man in the world, in the disciplines of the pristine
wars of the Romans.

JAMY: I say gud-day, Captain Fluellen.

FLUELLEN: God-den to your worship, good Captain James.

GOWER: How now Captain Macmorris, have you quit the
mines? Have the pioners given o'er?   77

MACMORRIS: By Chrish la! Tish ill done: the work ish give
over, the trompet sound the retreat. By my hand I swear, and
my father's soul, the work ish ill done; it ish give over. I
would have blowed up the town, so Chrish save me la! in an
hour: O tish ill done, tish ill done; by my hand tish ill done.

FLUELLEN: Captain Macmorris, I beseech you now, will you
voutsafe me, look you, a few disputations with you, as partly
touching or concerning the disciplines of the war, the Roman
wars, in the way of argument, look you, and friendly com-
munication; partly to satisfy my opinion, and partly for the
satisfaction, look you, of my mind, as touching the direction
of the military discipline; that is the point.   89

JAMY: It sall be vary gud, gud feith, gud captains bath; and I
sall quit you with gud leve, as I may pick occasion; that sall
I marry.

MACMORRIS: It is no time to discourse, so Chrish save me. The
day is hot, and the weather, and the wars, and the King, and
the dukes; it is no time to discourse, the town is beseeched.
And the trumpet call us to the breach, and we talk, and be
Chrish do nothing; 'tis shame for us all. So God sa' me, 'tis
shame to stand still; it is shame, by my hand. And there is
throats to be cut, and works to be done, and there ish nothing
done, so Chrish sa' me, la!   100

JAMY: By the mess, ere theise eyes of mine take themselves to
slomber, ay'll do gud service, or ay'll lig i' the grund for it; ay,
or go to death. And ay'll pay't as valorously as I may, that sall
I suerly do, that is the breff and the long. Marry, I wad full
fain hear some question 'tween you tway.

106–7 *Captain . . . nation.* Jorgensen suggests that Fluellen was going on to say ' "who is one of his majesty's captains". And he would have added, or implied that an Irish captain was not only a rare species, but one unqualified to talk of the "disciplines" of war'.

113 *use me*, treat me.

115 *derivation of my birth.* A notable Welsh characteristic in Shakespeare's day.

S.D. *A parley*, a trumpet call.

123 *to be required*, to be obtained, presents itself.

Is Fluellen—quarrelsome, conceited, pedantic, ignorant, earnest, dedicated, cocksure, genuine, argumentative, quick-tempered?

Is the purpose of this scene—to entertain with a comic clash of accents, to mount a satire against the Scots and Irish, to show the discords Henry had to face, to show the unity of his army in spite of the diversity of its individuals (i.e. 'many ways meet in one town'), to raise interest from introducing topical issue?

Before the gates of Harfleur

S.D. The Governor, soldiers, and citizens occupy the stage balcony or the musicians' room. Some summoning of the Governor to a parley by trumpets is required.

2 *parle*, parley.

4 *proud of destruction*, so misguided as to let their pride lead to the destruction of the town. Most editors interpret 'elated with the thought of death'. But the proverb 'pride goeth before destruction' (*Proverbs*, xvi. 18) may be involved. In any case Henry is condemning the townsfolk not praising their courage.

7 *battery*, assault.

8 *half-achieved*, half-captured.

FLUELLEN: Captain Macmorris, I think, look you, under your correction, there is not many of your nation—

MACMORRIS: Of my nation! What ish my nation? Ish a villain, and a bastard, and a knave, and a rascal—what ish my nation? Who talks of my nation?   110

FLUELLEN: Look you, if you take the matter otherwise than is meant, Captain Macmorris, peradventure I shall think you do not use me with that affability as in discretion you ought to use me, look you; being as good a man as yourself, both in the disciplines of war, and in the derivation of my birth, and in other particularities.

MACMORRIS: I do not know you so good a man as myself. So Chrish save me, I will cut off your head.

GOWER: Gentlemen both, you will mistake each other.

JAMY: Ah that's a foul fault.   [*A parley sounded* 120

GOWER: The town sounds a parley.

FLUELLEN: Captain Macmorris, when there is more better opportunity to be required, look you, I will be so bold as to tell you I know the disciplines of war; and there is an end.

[*Exeunt*

SCENE THREE

Enter KING HENRY *and all his train before the gates*

KING HENRY: How yet resolves the governor of the town?
This is the latest parle we will admit.
Therefore to our best mercy give yourselves,
Or like to men proud of destruction
Defy us to our worst. For as I am a soldier,
A name that in my thoughts becomes me best,
If I begin the battery once again,
I will not leave the half-achieved Harfleur

10   *gates of mercy*. Perhaps an allusion to the gates of Heaven. See *3 Henry VI*, I. iv, 177, 'Open thy gate of mercy, gracious God'.

11   *fleshed*, hardened to bloodshed.

12   *liberty . . . hand*, free to indulge in slaughter.

13   *With . . . hell*, with a conscience stretched wide enough to sanction hellish deeds.

15–21 *What . . . violation*, i.e. Henry will have no pity or responsibility for the brutalities.

15   *impious war*. Henry maintains that the French are impiously fighting against him the rightful king. Note the Latin phrase 'bellum impium' = civil war.

17   *smirched complexion*, (*a*) blackened features, (*b*) foul nature. *fell feats*, terrible deeds that accompany the devastation and ruin of a city.

22–3 *What . . . career*, what control can check evil licence once it is in headlong rush.

24   *bootless*, vainly, uselessly.

25   *enraged*, wildly violent.

26–7 *As . . . ashore*. Ironic. *Job*, xli. 1 'Canst thou draw out leviathan with an hook?'

26   *precepts*, written commands.
    Any response, reactions or movements among the citizens.

29   *Whiles . . . command*. Henry's conduct is strictly according to military code. He has allowed the besieged time to find out whether they may expect relief (ll. 44–7) and is about to mount a final assault which he believes will succeed. If his troops break into the city it would be impossible to control them when they are scattered throughout the town. He warns the Governor that he should surrender at once or the city may suffer the appalling horrors of sacking.

31   *contagious*, disease-carrying, noxious.

32   *heady*, headlong.

34   *blind*, heedless, raging.

38   *infants . . . pikes*. The massacre of the Innocents was frequently depicted in medieval and renaissance illustrations.

40   *break the clouds*, shatter the heavens.

40–1 *as . . . slaughtermen*. The massacre of the Innocents. See *Matt.* ii. 16–18.

Till in her ashes she lie buried.
The gates of mercy shall be all shut up, 10
And the fleshed soldier, rough and hard of heart,
In liberty of bloody hand shall range
With conscience wide as hell, mowing like grass
Your fresh-fair virgins, and your flowering infants.
What is it then to me, if impious war,
Arrayed in flames like to the prince of fiends,
Do with his smirched complexion all fell feats
Enlinked to waste and desolation?
What is 't to me, when you yourselves are cause,
If your pure maidens fall into the hand 20
Of hot and forcing violation?
What rein can hold licentious wickedness
When down the hill he holds his fierce career?
We may as bootless spend our vain command
Upon the enraged soldiers in their spoil,
As send precepts to the leviathan
To come ashore. Therefore, you men of Harfleur,
Take pity of your town and of your people,
Whiles yet my soldiers are in my command,
Whiles yet the cool and temperate wind of grace 30
O'erblows the filthy and contagious clouds
Of heady murder, spoil, and villany.
If not, why in a moment look to see
The blind and bloody soldier with foul hand
Defile the locks of your shrill-shrieking daughters;
Your fathers taken by the silver beards,
And their most reverend heads dashed to the walls;
Your naked infants spitted upon pikes,
Whiles the mad mothers with their howls confused
Do break the clouds, as did the wives of Jewry 40
At Herod's bloody-hunting slaughtermen.
What say you? Will you yield, and this avoid?

43 *guilty in defence*, (*a*) in holding out against the rightful king, (*b*) in refusing to surrender and so bringing about the destruction of the city and its inhabitants.

S.D. The Governor could speak from the balcony or the musicians' room or he could enter in the normal way.

50 *defensible*, able to defend ourselves.

51-3 *Come . . . French.* Exeter appointed Sir John Fastolf to take charge of the town.

54 *Use . . . all.* Shakespeare departs from Holinshed who recorded that the town was sacked.

55 *sickness*, dysentery and fevers.

58 *addrest*, prepared.

S.D. Flourish of trumpets accompanied by drums and fife.

Henry has been attacked on the grounds that this speech shows that he is neurotic, hysterical, obsessed with sexual outrage, and sadistic. On the other hand the purpose of this speech is to persuade the Governor to surrender, and Henry is at pains to convince him of his guilt, and to stress that the innocent and helpless will suffer by rape and murder. Miss Zimbardo notes the exaggerated rhetoric, the use of formal devices of style, and conventional diction. She adds 'The threat has nothing of passion in it. It cannot be mistaken for the personal threat of Henry or a reflection of his own feelings or desires, because its formalism marks it as part of a controlling order of which Henry himself is merely the instrument.'

Descriptions of the horrors of the sacking of cities were frequent in writers of the time. There were particularly frightful sackings involving murder and rape in the war in the Netherlands, notoriously at the sack of Bovaigne.

The palace at Rouen

S.D. Are the two occupied in any domestic activity? Gesture and action should be lively throughout with much pointing. Any properties required—stools, chairs, etc.? The French of this scene has been 'improved' in spelling, gender, and agreements, and there are a few other emendations, but it has not been fully corrected.

Shakespeare may have assumed that his audiences knew that Katharine as Henry's bride was one of the terms under discussion.

Or guilty in defence, be thus destroyed?

Enter Governor

GOVERNOR: Our expectation hath this day an end.
The Dauphin, whom of succours we entreated,
Returns us that his powers are yet not ready
To raise so great a siege. Therefore great King,
We yield our town and lives to thy soft mercy.
Enter our gates; dispose of us and ours,
For we no longer are defensible.   50
KING HENRY: Open your gates. Come uncle Exeter,
Go you and enter Harfleur; there remain,
And fortify it strongly 'gainst the French.
Use mercy to them all. For us, dear uncle,
The winter coming on and sickness growing
Upon our soldiers, we will retire to Calais.
Tonight in Harfleur will we be your guest,
Tomorrow for the march are we addrest.
                   [*Flourish. The King and his train enter the town*

SCENE FOUR

The FRENCH KING'S *palace*
Enter KATHARINE *and* ALICE

KATHARINE: Alice, tu as été en Angleterre, et tu bien parles le
langage.
ALICE: Un peu, madame.
KATHARINE: Je te prie m'enseignez; il faut que j'apprenne à
parler. Comment appelez-vous la main en Anglais?
ALICE: La main elle est appelée de hand.
KATHARINE: De hand. Et les doigts?
ALICE: Les doigts, ma foi, j'oublie les doigts; mais je me
souviendrai. Les doigts, je pense qu'ils sont appelés de fingres,
oui de fingres.   10

26   *bilbow*, (*a*) bilbo, a sword, (*b*) bilbo(es) chain(s) fastened to a
      prisoner's ankles.

30, 33 *nick*, sin. Perhaps an early glance at 'nick' = devil though the
        N.E.D. gives 1643 as its earliest appearance in print.

KATHARINE: La main, de hand; les doigts, de fingres. Je pense
que je suis le bon écolier; j'ai gagné deux mots d'Anglais
vitement. Comment appelez-vous les ongles?

ALICE: Les ongles, nous les appelons de nails.

KATHARINE: De nails. Ecoute; dites-moi, si je parle bien: de
hand, de fingres, et de nails.

ALICE: C'est bien dit madame, il est fort bon Anglais.

KATHARINE: Dites-moi l'Anglais pour le bras.

ALICE: De arm, madame.

KATHARINE: Et le coude?   20

ALICE: D'elbow.

KATHARINE: D'elbow. Je m'en fais la répétition de tous les
mots que vous m'avez appris dès à présent.

ALICE: Il est trop difficile madame, comme je pense.

KATHARINE: Excuse moi Alice; écoute: de hand, de fingres, de
nails, de arma, de bilbow.

ALICE: D'elbow madame.

KATHARINE: O Seigneur Dieu, je m'en oublie d'elbow. Comment appelez-vous le col?

ALICE: De nick, madame.   30

KATHARINE: De nick. Et le menton?

ALICE: De chin.

KATHARINE: De sin. Le col, de nick; le menton, de sin.

ALICE: Oui. Sauf votre honneur, en vérité, vous prononcez les
mots aussi droit que les natifs d'Angleterre.

KATHARINE: Je ne doute point d'apprendre, par la grace de
Dieu, et en peu de temps.

ALICE: N'avez-vous pas déjà oublié ce que je vous ai en-
seigné?

KATHARINE: Non, je reciterai à vous promptement: de hand,
de fingres, de mails,—   41

ALICE: De nails, madame.

KATHARINE: De nails, de arm, de ilbow.

ALICE: Sauf votre honneur, d'elbow.

46   *robe.* The Folio has 'roba', whore. See *2 Henry IV*, III. ii, 20.

48   *De . . . count.* Near in sound to obscene French words.
       Why was this scene introduced—because it was expected by the
       audience as part of the story (see Appendix: Sources), to relieve
       the tension after the previous scene by comedy and female society,
       to set the stage for the wooing scene to follow, to establish
       Katharine's respectability, i.e. that she is not just the spoil of the
       conqueror, to show the beginning of another action 'having full
       reference to one consent'?
       The lesson and the unseemly joke at the end apparently derives
       from French farces. Shakespeare's heroines are broad-minded and
       at times aware of coarseness, but like Katharine they deal firmly
       and sharply with anything that is immodest.

The palace at Rouen

s.d.   A formal ceremonial entry. Any properties required—throne,
       stools, chairs, maps, etc.?
s.d.   *Bretagne.* Some editors have 'Bourbon' from the Quarto; but this
       was due to cast reduction in the latter.
  1   *passed . . . Somme,* i.e. on his withdrawal to Calais.
2–4   *And . . . people.* Is the Constable—despairing, impatient, chafing,
       restless, desperate, frustrated?
  4   *vineyards . . . people,* i.e. give up our civilized life to savages.
  5   *sprays of us,* offshoots of us French.
  6   *The . . . luxury,* the dregs of our ancestors' lust.
  7   *scions . . . stock,* shoots grafted on to wild stocks, i.e. the offspring
       of intermarriage between Norsemen and French.
  8   *spirt,* sprout.
  9   *grafters,* trees from which the shoots were taken, i.e. the French.
 10   *Normans . . . bastards.* Emphatic order.

 13   *slobbery,* sodden.
 14   *nook-shotten,* riddled with inlets and bays. Bretagne is con-
       temptuous.

KATHARINE: Ainsi, dis-je; d'elbow, de nick, et de sin. Comment appelez-vous le pied et la robe?

ALICE: De foot, madame; et de count.

KATHARINE: De foot et de count! O Seigneur Dieu ils sont mots de son mauvais, corruptible, gros, et impudique, et non pour les dames d'honneur d'user. Je ne voudrais prononcer ces mots devant les seigneurs de France pour tout le monde. Foh, le foot et le count! Néanmoins, je reciterai une autre fois ma leçon ensemble: d'hand, de fingres, de nails, d'arm, d'elbow, de nick, de sin, de foot, de count. 54

ALICE: Excellent, madame!

KATHARINE: C'est assez pour une fois: allons-nous à diner.

[Exeunt

SCENE FIVE

Enter the KING OF FRANCE, *the* DAUPHIN, *the* DUKE OF BRETAGNE, *the* CONSTABLE OF FRANCE, *and others*

FRENCH KING: 'Tis certain he hath passed the river Somme.

CONSTABLE: And if he be not fought withal, my lord,
Let us not live in France; let us quit all,
And give our vineyards to a barbarous people.

DAUPHIN: O Dieu vivant! Shall a few sprays of us,
The emptying of our fathers' luxury,
Our scions, put in wild and savage stock,
Spirt up so suddenly into the clouds,
And overlook their grafters?

BRETAGNE: Normans, but bastard Normans, Norman bastards.
Mort de ma vie! If they march along 11
Unfought withal, but I will sell my dukedom,
To buy a slobbery and a dirty farm
In that nook-shotten isle of Albion.

15   *Dieu . . . mettle.* Is it in fact from the God of Battles?

17   *despite,* contempt. *pale,* (*a*) watery, (*b*) angry.

18   *frowns,* (*a*) anger, (*b*) rain clouds that hide the sun. See *A Mid-
      summer Night's Dream,* II. i, 103–5. *sodden water,* beer.

19   *A . . . jades,* a mere drink for hard ridden nags. *barley-broth,* beer.

20   *Decoct,* (*a*) warm, (*b*) infuse.

21   *quick,* lively. *spirited with wine.* The Constable regards wine as
      vital to culture (l. 4) and spirit.

23   *roping,* congealing, slow-trickling.

25   *Sweat . . . fields,* vigorously campaign with fine young soldiers.

26   *in,* in the quality of.

28–9 *Our . . . out,* we are no longer capable of begetting spirited and
      vigorous offspring.
          The emphasis has been on the English breed with a supporting
      theme of fertility despite the disadvantage of climate and lack of
      wine.

32–5 *They . . . runaways,* they mockingly tell us to go to England as
      dancing-masters to teach such leaping and running step dances,
      because our only virtue is in our heels and we are excellent at
      running away.
          French dancing masters were fashionable in Elizabethan
      England.

33   *lavoltas high.* The lavolta was a dance in three-four time in which
      a turn in two steps was followed by a high leap. *swift corantos.* A
      dance in two-four time with a running step.

34   *grace,* (*a*) skill, (*b*) saving grace. *in our heels,* (*a*) in dancing, (*b*) in
      showing a clean pair of heels.

35   *lofty runaways,* lofty (lavoltas) runaways (corantos). A neat
      summing up of the ladies' sarcasm.
          Is the Dauphin—petulant, ridiculous, exasperated, plaintive,
      effeminate, foppish, resentful?

40–5 *Charles . . . Charolois.* This bede-roll of names of French chivalry
      is typical of epic style.

47   *For . . . seats,* for the sake of your mighty positions. *quit you,* acquit
      yourselves.

CONSTABLE: Dieu de batailles where have they this mettle?
  Is not their climate foggy, raw, and dull,
  On whom, as in despite, the sun looks pale,
  Killing their fruit with frowns? Can sodden water,
  A drench for sur-reined jades, their barley-broth,
  Decoct their cold blood to such valiant heat?   20
  And shall our quick blood, spirited with wine,
  Seem frosty? O, for honour of our land,
  Let us not hang like roping icicles
  Upon our houses' thatch, whiles a more frosty people
  Sweat drops of gallant youth in our rich fields—
  Poor we may call them in their native lords.
DAUPHIN: By faith and honour,
  Our madams mock at us, and plainly say
  Our mettle is bred out, and they will give
  Their bodies to the lust of English youth   30
  To new-store France with bastard warriors.
BRETAGNE: They bid us to the English dancing-schools,
  And teach lavoltas high and swift corantos,
  Saying our grace is only in our heels,
  And that we are most lofty runaways.
FRENCH KING: Where is Montjoy the herald? Speed him hence,
  Let him greet England with our sharp defiance.
  Up princes, and with spirit of honour edged
  More sharper than your swords, hie to the field.
  Charles Delabreth, high constable of France;   40
  You Dukes of Orleans, Bourbon, and of Berri,
  Alençon, Brabant, Bar, and Burgundy;
  Jacques Chatillon, Rambures, Vaudemont,
  Beaumont, Grandpré, Roussi, and Faulconbridge,
  Foix, Lestrale, Bouciqualt, and Charolois;
  High dukes, great princes, barons, lords, and knights,
  For your great seats now quit you of great shames.
  Bar Harry England, that sweeps through our land

52 *The . . . upon.* This line is a translation of a Latin verse condemned as strained and inapt by early writers. Is it to render the French King ridiculous by putting an indecorous image in his mouth, is its indecorum meant to show his contempt for Henry, or is it a further example of disorder among the French? *rheum*, spittle, phlegm.

55 *becomes the great*, attitude is worthy of a great man.

56-7 *Sorry . . . march*, i.e. there would be greater glory in defeating a fitter and larger army. The Constable's remark also indicates the achievement of the English if they win.

60 *for achievement*, (*a*) to conclude the matter, (*b*) instead of an honourable encounter (Arden).

63 *willing*, of his free will.

64-6 *Prince . . . us.* This agrees with Holinshed, but Shakespeare takes him to Agincourt.

This scene has links with III. i. Both deal with the themes of bread and 'pasture', both have royal speeches to army leaders. On the other hand there are balanced contrasts: noble birth—bastardy, breed—degeneracy, action—inaction, leadership—indecision. Henry precisely instructs each man how to attune himself to battle; the French King recounts a list of illustrious names and tells their owners to rush in disorderly fashion on the English.

English camp

S.D. Business-like, purposeful entries from opposite sides.

2 *bridge.* The bridge over the Ternoise was captured by the English advance forces two days before Agincourt. Henry's main army crossed it on the next day.

3 *services*, deeds of arms.

5 *Exeter.* For clarity and dramatic economy Shakespeare retains Exeter throughout the play. According to Holinshed he was not at the capture of the bridge.

6 *magnanimous*, great-souled. Magnanimity was the most highly praised virtue.

6-7 *Agamemnon.* King of Argos, and leader of the Greeks at Troy.

With pennons painted in the blood of Harfleur.
Rush on his host, as doth the melted snow   50
Upon the valleys, whose low vassal seat
The Alps doth spit and void his rheum upon.
Go down upon him, you have power enough,
And in a captive chariot into Rouen
Bring him our prisoner.
CONSTABLE: This becomes the great.
  Sorry am I his numbers are so few,
  His soldiers sick and famished in their march,
  For I am sure when he shall see our army
  He'll drop his heart into the sink of fear,
  And for achievement offer us his ransom.   60
FRENCH KING: Therefore lord Constable, haste on Montjoy,
  And let him say to England that we send
  To know what willing ransom he will give.
  Prince Dauphin, you shall stay with us in Rouen.
DAUPHIN: Not so, I do beseech your majesty.
FRENCH KING: Be patient, for you shall remain with us.
  Now forth, lord Constable and princes all,
  And quickly bring us word of England's fall.   [*Exeunt*

SCENE SIX

Enter GOWER *and* FLUELLEN, *meeting*

GOWER: How now Captain Fluellen, come you from the
  bridge?
FLUELLEN: I assure you there is very excellent services committed at the bridge.
GOWER: Is the Duke of Exeter safe?
FLUELLEN: The Duke of Exeter is as magnanimous as Agamemnon, and a man that I love and honour with my soul, and

11 *aunchient lieutenant.* Something like first lieutenant.

12–14 *he . . . service.* Fluellen presumably was deceived by Pistol's vocal valiancy, which prompts the reference to Mark Antony.

13 *Mark Antony.* See *Julius Cæsar* and *Antony and Cleopatra.* Marcus Antonius whose oratory incited the Romans to drive out Brutus whom he later defeated in battle. He ruled over Egypt with Cleopatra, but was killed at the battle of Actium against Octavius.

24 *buxom,* sturdy.

25–7 *giddy . . . stone.* The Roman goddess Fortuna was a popular subject for painters and poets of the period. Fluellen's description gives an adequate account of her. Baldwin claims that Fluellen's version is drawn from a description well-known as an example of faulty reasoning, and as a demonstration that men's misfortunes are due to their own follies. Bardolph therefore had only himself to blame.

25 *furious,* cruel.

34 *poet.* No particular poet seems to be intended. Fluellen may be referring to an emblem where moralizing verses were written below a painting or woodcut of the goddess.

36 *Fortune . . . foe.* An echo of the ballad 'Fortune, my foe, why dost thou frown on me?'

37 *stolen a pax.* Henry had issued orders expressly prohibiting the robbing of churches. Holinshed records that a soldier was executed by strangling for stealing a 'pyx', a box containing

my heart, and my duty, and my life, and my living, and my uttermost power. He is not—God be praised and blessed—any hurt in the world; but keeps the bridge most valiantly, with excellent discipline. There is an aunchient lieutenant there at the pridge, I think in my very conscience he is as valiant a man as Mark Antony; and he is a man of no estimation in the world, but I did see him do as gallant service. 14

GOWER: What do you call him?

FLUELLEN: He is called Aunchient Pistol.

GOWER: I know him not.

Enter PISTOL

FLUELLEN: Here is the man.

PISTOL: Captain, I thee beseech to do me favours.
The Duke of Exeter doth love thee well. 20

FLUELLEN: Ay, I praise God, and I have merited some love at his hands.

PISTOL: Bardolph, a soldier firm and sound of heart,
And of buxom valour, hath by cruel fate,
And giddy Fortune's furious fickle wheel,
That goddess blind,
That stands upon the rolling restless stone— 27

FLUELLEN: By your patience, Aunchient Pistol. Fortune is painted blind, with a muffler afore her eyes, to signify to you that Fortune is blind; and she is painted also with a wheel, to signify to you, which is the moral of it, that she is turning, and inconstant, and mutability, and variation; and her foot, look you, is fixed upon a spherical stone, which rolls, and rolls, and rolls. In good truth, the poet makes a most excellent description of it. Fortune is an excellent moral.

PISTOL: Fortune is Bardolph's foe, and frowns on him;
For he hath stolen a pax, and hanged must a be.
A damned death.
Let gallows gape for dog, let man go free,

consecrated wafers. *pax*, a small metal plate with a crucifix or picture of Christ on it, formerly given to the congregation to kiss during mass as a sign of peace.

41   *doom*, judgment, sentence.

54   *figo*. A coarse expression of dislike often emphasized by putting the thumb into the mouth.

56   *fig of Spain*. A more emphatic 'figo'.

57   *Very good*. Fluellen shows remarkable restraint. Bardolph and Nym now disappear from the play. Why are they killed off—to exemplify Henry's justice, to remove all traces of his wild days, to remove unprincipled soldiers who were not in unity with the army?

58   *arrant counterfeit*, out and out false.

59   *bawd*, brothel-keeper.

62–3   *when . . . serve*, i.e. I'll settle that at the right time.

64   *gull*, stupid fellow.

65–6   *to . . . soldier*, in order to gain honour under the pose of a soldier.

68   *rote*, heart. *services*, actions, combats. *sconce*, fort.

69   *came off*, acquitted himself, behaved.

70–1   *what . . . on*, what was the situation of the enemy.

71   *and . . . war*, and this they learn off in the correct military jargon.

72   *new-tuned*, newly coined.

72–3   *beard . . . cut*, beard cut to imitate the General's style. Perhaps a reference to the Cadiz beards worn by Essex and his followers after the capture of Cadiz.

73   *horrid . . . camp*, rough battle-dress.

73–4   *among . . . wits*, where ale flows freely and soaks men's brains.

And let not hemp his wind-pipe suffocate.   40
But Exeter hath given the doom of death
For pax of little price.
Therefore go speak, the Duke will hear thy voice:
And let not Bardolph's vital thread be cut
With edge of penny cord and vile reproach.
Speak captain for his life, and I will thee requite.

FLUELLEN: Aunchient Pistol, I do partly understand your meaning.

PISTOL: Why then rejoice therefore.   49

FLUELLEN: Certainly aunchient, it is not a thing to rejoice at. For if, look you, he were my brother, I would desire the Duke to use his good pleasure, and put him to execution; for discipline ought to be used.

PISTOL: Die and be damned, and figo for thy friendship!

FLUELLEN: It is well.

PISTOL: The fig of Spain!   [*Exit*

FLUELLEN: Very good.

GOWER: Why, this is an arrant counterfeit rascal; I remember him now; a bawd, a cutpurse.   59

FLUELLEN: I'll assure you, a uttered as prave words at the pridge as you shall see in a summer's day. But it is very well; what he has spoke to me, that is well, I warrant you, when time is serve.

GOWER: Why, 'tis a gull, a fool, a rogue, that now and then goes to the wars, to grace himself at his return into London under the form of a soldier. And such fellows are perfect in the great commanders' names; and they will learn you by rote where services were done; at such and such a sconce, at such a breach, at such a convoy; who came off bravely, who was shot, who disgraced, what terms the enemy stood on; and this they con perfectly in the phrase of war, which they trick up with new-tuned oaths. And what a beard of the general's cut, and a horrid suit of the camp will do among

75-6   *slanders . . . age*, wickedness that shames our times.

76   *mistook*, deceived.

        A further condemnation of the offscourings of war, and an
        attack on those criminals who use war for their own private gains,
        and their rejection by the professional soldier.

79   *find . . . coat*, find a fault in him, find a chance to show him up.
        Proverbial.

81   *from the pridge*. Fluellen apparently is intercepted.

s.d.   *Drum . . . Soldiers*. Perhaps a book-keeper's note indicating that
        the soldiers are to appear exhausted, weatherworn, with be-
        draggled clothes and no plumes.

86   *passages*, deeds.

95   *bubukles*, abscesses, carbuncles. *whelks*, pimples.

96   *lips . . . nose*. Perhaps a cleft upper lip.

97   *nose is executed*, slit as he stood in the pillory before being hanged
        (Dover Wilson).

98   *his*, its.

        Should Henry show any reaction, or acknowledge that he
        knows Bardolph? Why is this brought to Henry's notice—so that
        he may confirm that the law should be enforced with no
        favouritism?

103-4   *for . . . winner*. Is Henry guided by policy rather than humanity?

foaming bottles and ale-washed wits is wonderful to be
thought on. But you must learn to know such slanders of the
age, or else you may be marvellously mistook.   76
FLUELLEN: I tell you what, Captain Gower; I do perceive he is
not the man that he would gladly make show to the world he
is; if I find a hole in his coat, I will tell him my mind. [*Drum
heard.*] Hark you, the King is coming, and I must speak with
him from the pridge.   81

Drum and colours. Enter KING HENRY, *and his poor
Soldiers,* GLOUCESTER

God pless your majesty.
KING HENRY: How now Fluellen, cam'st thou from the bridge?
FLUELLEN: Ay, so please your majesty. The Duke of Exeter has
very gallantly maintained the pridge. The French is gone off,
look you, and there is gallant and most prave passages.
Marry, th' athversary was have possession of the pridge, but
he is enforced to retire, and the Duke of Exeter is master of
the pridge. I can tell your majesty, the Duke is a prave man.
KING HENRY: What men have you lost, Fluellen?   90
FLUELLEN: The perdition of th' athversary hath been very great,
reasonable great. Marry for my part, I think the Duke hath
lost never a man, but one that is like to be executed for robbing a church, one Bardolph, if your majesty know the man.
His face is all bubukles, and whelks, and knobs, and flames o'
fire; and his lips blows at his nose, and it is like a coal of fire,
sometimes plue, and sometimes red; but his nose is executed,
and his fire's out.   98
KING HENRY: We would have all such offenders so cut off.
And we give express charge, that in our marches through the
country there be nothing compelled from the villages, nothing
taken but paid for, none of the French upbraided or abused in
disdainful language; for when lenity and cruelty play for a
kingdom, the gentler gamester is the soonest winner.   104

s.D. *Tucket.* A fanfare of trumpets.

105 *You . . . habit.* Montjoy is insolent. *habit,* a herald's tabard or sleeveless coat.

106 *Well . . . thee.* A light playing on 'know'.

110– *Say . . . pronounced.* Should Montjoy read from a scroll or declaim
25 from memory? Why is this in prose?

111 *advantage,* seizing the right moment.

113– *bruise . . . ripe,* i.e. squeeze a boil until it was ready.
14

114 *upon our cue,* at the right time, when our turn has come.

116 *admire our sufferance,* wonder at our patience.

118– *disgrace . . . digested,* humiliation we have swallowed.
19

119– *which . . . under,* which to repay in adequate quantity would
20 overload his slender resources.

121 *muster,* roll, number (of subjects).
    Do the 'poor soldiers' react at these insults?

124–5 *he . . . pronounced,* he is guilty of misleading his troops whose doom is sealed.
    The French King's message is inconsequential, and displays weakness and indecision: we were not ready to face Henry in battle, now we are. We demand ransom and compensation which he is too impoverished to satisfy, we formally defy him, and add that he has betrayed his men.

128 *Montjoy.* Actually the title of the Chief Herald. Shakespeare may have had in mind Montjoy, a Frenchman with whose family he lodged.

132 *impeachment,* challenge, hindrance.

134 *craft and vantage,* skill and who has the initiative.

Act Three, Scene Six

Tucket. Enter MONTJOY

MONTJOY: You know me by my habit.

KING HENRY: Well then I know thee. What shall I know of thee?

MONTJOY: My master's mind.

KING HENRY: Unfold it.   109

MONTJOY: Thus says my King. Say thou to Harry of England, Though we seemed dead, we did but sleep; advantage is a better soldier than rashness. Tell him we could have rebuked him at Harfleur, but that we thought not good to bruise an injury till it were full ripe. Now we speak upon our cue, and our voice is imperial. England shall repent his folly, see his weakness, and admire our sufferance. Bid him therefore consider of his ransom, which must proportion the losses we have borne, the subjects we have lost, the disgrace we have digested; which in weight to re-answer, his pettiness would bow under. For our losses, his exchequer is too poor; for th' effusion of our blood, the muster of his kingdom too faint a number; and for our disgrace, his own person kneeling at our feet but a weak and worthless satisfaction. To this add defiance: and tell him for conclusion, he hath betrayed his followers, whose condemnation is pronounced. So far my King and master; so much my office.

KING HENRY: What is thy name? I know thy quality.

MONTJOY: Montjoy.

KING HENRY: Thou dost thy office fairly. Turn thee back,
And tell thy King I do not seek him now,   130
But could be willing to march on to Calais
Without impeachment: for to say the sooth,
Though 'tis no wisdom to confess so much
Unto an enemy of craft and vantage,
My people are with sickness much enfeebled,
My numbers lessened, and those few I have

148   *There's ... labour.* Holinshed states that Henry gave Montjoy a 'princely reward'.

Henry takes the gift from an attendant.

Henry insists that in spite of the condition of his men, which Montjoy can see, he has no intention of surrendering and will give battle if challenged.

Is Henry prudent, boastful, a strategist, foolhardy, diplomatic, provident for his men, magnanimous?

Almost no better than so many French;
Who when they were in health, I tell thee herald,
I thought upon one pair of English legs
Did march three Frenchmen. Yet forgive me God,   140
That I do brag thus. This your air of France
Hath blown that vice in me; I must repent.
Go therefore tell thy master here I am;
My ransom is this frail and worthless trunk;
My army but a weak and sickly guard.
Yet God before, tell him we will come on,
Though France himself and such another neighbour
Stand in our way. There's for thy labour Montjoy.
Go bid thy master well advise himself.
If we may pass, we will; if we be hindered,   150
We shall your tawny ground with your red blood
Discolour. And so Montjoy, fare you well.
The sum of all our answer is but this:
We would not seek a battle as we are,
Nor as we are, we say we will not shun it.
So tell your master.
MONTJOY: I shall deliver so. Thanks to your highness.   [*Exit*
GLOUCESTER: I hope they will not come upon us now.
KING HENRY: We are in God's hand, brother, not in theirs.
March to the bridge; it now draws toward night.   160
Beyond the river we'll encamp ourselves,
And on tomorrow bid them march away.   [*Exeunt*

The French camp at Agincourt

S.D.   They enter conversing. The conversation suggests that they are tense and edgy. Are they in armour? In this scene Orleans, the Constable, and the Dauphin are individually characterized.

9–10   *You . . . world.* Is Orleans being tactful or trying to forestall a long speech in praise of the Dauphin's horse?

12   *pasterns.* Here legs or hoofs. *Ca, ha.* The Folio has ch' ha', perhaps a call to his horse.

12–13   *He . . . hairs.* The comparison suggests a tennis ball, hardly an apt image for this horse, the 'Pegasus'.

13   *bounds.* The 'bound' was the term for a series of even jumps on the same spot.

14   *Pegasus.* In classical myth the winged horse which sprang from the blood of the gorgon Medusa after Perseus cut off her head. *les narines de feu.* A medieval addition to the classical figure.

15–16   *the . . . it.* Hippocrene, the fountain of the Muses sprang from Mt. Helicon where Pegasus struck it with his hoof.

17   *pipe of Hermes.* Hermes, the Greek messenger god, charmed to sleep Argus the watchful hundred-eyed monster.

18–19   *colour . . . ginger.* The colour of a horse was held to indicate the elements in its make-up and hence its temperament. If the element fire predominated, then its colour was bright reddish brown or sorrel, if air, then a bay colour.

19–20   *a . . . Perseus.* Perseus was in some versions of the myth the rider of Pegasus. After killing Medusa he rescued Andromeda from the sea-serpent which was turned to stone at the sight of Medusa's head, married her, and founded Mycenae.

SCENE SEVEN

Enter the CONSTABLE OF FRANCE, *the* LORD RAMBURES,
ORLEANS, DAUPHIN, *with others*

CONSTABLE: Tut, I have the best armour of the world. Would
it were day!

ORLEANS: You have an excellent armour; but let my horse have
his due.

CONSTABLE: It is the best horse of Europe.

ORLEANS: Will it never be morning?

DAUPHIN: My Lord of Orleans, and my lord high Constable,
you talk of horse and armour?

ORLEANS: You are as well provided of both as any prince in the
world.   10

DAUPHIN: What a long night is this! I will not change my
horse with any that treads but on four pasterns. Ça, ha! He
bounds from the earth, as if his entrails were hairs; le cheval
volant, the Pegasus, chez les narines de feu. When I bestride
him, I soar, I am a hawk: he trots the air; the earth sings
when he touches it; the basest horn of his hoof is more musical
than the pipe of Hermes.

ORLEANS: He's of the colour of the nutmeg.   18

DAUPHIN: And of the heat of the ginger. It is a beast for
Perseus. He is pure air and fire; and the dull elements of earth
and water never appear in him, but only in patient stillness
while his rider mounts him. He is indeed a horse, and all other
jades you may call beasts.

CONSTABLE: Indeed my lord, it is a most absolute and excellent
horse.

DAUPHIN: It is the prince of palfreys; his neigh is like the bid-
ding of a monarch, and his countenance enforces homage.

ORLEANS: No more, cousin.   28

DAUPHIN: Nay, the man hath no wit that cannot from the

30   *lodging,* going to bed.
30–1 *vary deserved praise.* 'Vary' was a term in rhetoric for amplifying
a theme by adding apt figures of speech, quotations, allusions, and
illustrations, to give delight. A 'praise' was also a rhetorical term
for a prescribed arrangement of the good qualities of the subject.
The Dauphin's 'varying' is indecorous, it is excessive and out of
harmony with its subject. His companions point out that such
praise is more applicable to his lady-love, and ridicule the matter
with bawdy insinuations.
33   *sovereign . . . on.* A quibble, 'reason' was the sovereign of human
attributes.
34   *sovereign's sovereign.* See l. 26.
36   *functions,* occupations.

42   *prescript,* apt, precise.

43   *particular,* i.e. having only one lover.

45   *shrewdly,* (*a*) severely, (*b*) like a shrewish woman.

47   *bridled,* (*a*) as a horse, (*b*) as a shrewish woman punished by having
to wear a bridle.

49   *kern of Ireland,* light-armed Irish soldier. *French hose,* loose wide
breeches.
49–50 *strait strossers,* (*a*) tight trousers, (*b*) bare-legged.
51   *horsemanship.* Possibly a quibble on 'whores'.

55   *jade,* loose woman.
56–7 *my . . . hair,* i.e. the Constable's mistress is so old that she wears
false hair.

60–1 *Le . . . bourbier. 2 Pet.* ii. 22. This sudden use of French is perhaps
a sign of intense violent feeling. See ll. 12–14, IV. v, 1–5. It could
also serve to remind the audience of the nationality of the
speakers.
62–3 *Yet . . . purpose.* The Constable and the Dauphin are now openly
at odds.

rising of the lark to the lodging of the lamb vary deserved
praise on my palfrey. It is a theme as fluent as the sea. Turn
the sands into eloquent tongues, and my horse is argument
for them all. 'Tis a subject for a sovereign to reason on, and
for a sovereign's sovereign to ride on; and for the world,
familiar to us and unknown, to lay apart their particular
functions and wonder at him. I once writ a sonnet in his
praise and began thus: 'Wonder of nature,'—

ORLEANS: I have heard a sonnet begin so to one's mistress.

DAUPHIN: Then did they imitate that which I composed to my
courser, for my horse is my mistress.   40

ORLEANS: Your mistress bears well.

DAUPHIN: Me well, which is the prescript praise and perfection
of a good and particular mistress.

CONSTABLE: Nay, for methought yesterday your mistress
shrewdly shook your back.

DAUPHIN: So perhaps did yours.

CONSTABLE: Mine was not bridled.

DAUPHIN: O then belike she was old and gentle, and you rode
like a kern of Ireland, your French hose off, and in your strait
strossers.   50

CONSTABLE: You have good judgment in horsemanship.

DAUPHIN: Be warned by me, then. They that ride so and ride
not warily, fall into foul bogs. I had rather have my horse to
my mistress.

CONSTABLE: I had as lief have my mistress a jade.

DAUPHIN: I tell thee Constable, my mistress wears his own
hair.

CONSTABLE: I could make as true a boast as that if I had a sow
to my mistress.   59

DAUPHIN: 'Le chien est retourné à son propre vomissement, et
la truie lavée au bourbier.' Thou makest use of any thing.

CONSTABLE: Yet do I not use my horse for my mistress, or any
such proverb so little kin to the purpose.

65   *stars*. Perhaps a form of ornamentation indicating feats of arms. Rambures attempts to turn the conversation.

67   *Some . . . hope*, i.e. that he will lose some of his honours.

68   *And . . . want*, and yet I shall not lack fame.

72   *brags dismounted*, i.e. rid your horse of some of your extravagant boasts you have saddled him with.

76–7   *faced . . . way*, (*a*) put out of countenance, shamed (for boasting), (*b*) driven away.

77   *fain*, gladly.

79–80 *go . . . prisoners*, bet me that I won't capture twenty prisoners.

81   *go to hazard*, (*a*) wager, (*b*) endanger.

85   *to . . . English*, i.e. he is a fierce boaster.

86   *I . . . kills*, i.e. he will not kill anyone. Heavily sarcastic charge of weakness.

87   *By . . . prince*. Orleans defends the Dauphin.

88   *tread out the oath*, (*a*) obliterate the oath, (*b*) thresh the oats, i.e. sift out the truth.

89   *active*, brisk, energetic.

90   *Doing . . . doing*. The Constable's sarcasm perhaps condemns the Dauphin for much doing but no achievement.

92–3   *He . . . still*, i.e. 'harmless'.

RAMBURES: My lord Constable, the armour that I saw in your tent tonight, are those stars or suns upon it?

CONSTABLE: Stars my lord.

DAUPHIN: Some of them will fall tomorrow, I hope.

CONSTABLE: And yet my sky shall not want.

DAUPHIN: That may be, for you bear a many superfluously, and 'twere more honour some were away.   70

CONSTABLE: Ev'n as your horse bears your praises, who would trot as well, were some of your brags dismounted.

DAUPHIN: Would I were able to load him with his desert. Will it never be day? I will trot tomorrow a mile, and my way shall be paved with English faces.

CONSTABLE: I will not say so, for fear I should be faced out of my way. But I would it were morning, for I would fain be about the ears of the English.

RAMBURES: Who will go to hazard with me for twenty prisoners?   80

CONSTABLE: You must first go yourself to hazard, ere you have them.

DAUPHIN: 'Tis midnight, I'll go arm myself.   [*Exit*

ORLEANS: The Dauphin longs for morning.

RAMBURES: He longs to eat the English.

CONSTABLE: I think he will eat all he kills.

ORLEANS: By the white hand of my lady, he's a gallant prince.

CONSTABLE: Swear by her foot, that she may tread out the oath.

ORLEANS: He is simply the most active gentleman of France.

CONSTABLE: Doing is activity, and he will still be doing.   90

ORLEANS: He never did harm, that I heard of.

CONSTABLE: Nor will do none tomorrow. He will keep that good name still.

ORLEANS: I know him to be valiant.

CONSTABLE: I was told that by one that knows him better than you.

ORLEANS: What's he?

98–9   *he . . . it.* Fatuous piece of boasting.

101–2   *Never . . . lackey,* his servant is the only one whom the Dauphin has had the courage to strike.

102–3   *hooded . . . bate,* valour concealed like a hawk's head with a hood, and like a hawk when uncovered it will give a flutter. It will not soar to the high pitch of courage. 'Bate' also means 'to dwindle'.

104   *Ill . . . well.* The proverb makes use of a quibble 'well': 'will'. See *Merry Wives of Windsor*, I. iii, 46–7.

105   *cap,* reply, follow up with, outdo.

105–6   *There . . . friendship.* A common proverb. See *Twelfth Night*, V. i, 10–20. The Constable suggests that Orleans is flattering the Dauphin.

109–   *Well . . . devil'.* That shot was well placed indeed for your friend
    11   may represent the devil and I will attack the very point of your proverb by giving the devil his due with 'A pox of the devil'.

114   *shot over,* shot beyond the target.

115   *overshot,* beaten, out-shot.

123   *peevish,* thoughtless, foolish.

124–5   *to . . . knowledge,* to wander bewilderedly with his ignorant followers beyond the range of his powers of understanding.

126   *apprehension,* (*a*) common sense, (*b*) fear.

128–9   *for . . . head-pieces,* i.e. there is no weight of brains.

CONSTABLE: Marry he told me so himself, and he said he cared not who knew it.

ORLEANS: He needs not, it is no hidden virtue in him.　　100

CONSTABLE: By my faith sir, but it is. Never any body saw it but his lackey. 'Tis a hooded valour, and when it appears, it will bate.

ORLEANS: Ill will never said well.

CONSTABLE: I will cap that proverb with 'There is flattery in friendship'.

ORLEANS: And I will take up that with 'Give the devil his due'.

CONSTABLE: Well placed: there stands your friend for the devil. Have at the very eye of that proverb with 'A pox of the devil'.　　111

ORLEANS: You are the better at proverbs, by how much 'A fool's bolt is soon shot'.

CONSTABLE: You have shot over.

ORLEANS: 'Tis not the first time you were overshot.

Enter a Messenger

MESSENGER: My lord high Constable, the English lie within fifteen hundred paces of your tents.

CONSTABLE: Who hath measured the ground?

MESSENGER: The Lord Grandpré.　　119

CONSTABLE: A valiant and most expert gentleman. Would it were day! Alas poor Harry of England, he longs not for the dawning as we do.

ORLEANS: What a wretched and peevish fellow is this King of England, to mope with his fat-brained followers so far out of his knowledge!

CONSTABLE: If the English had any apprehension, they would run away.

ORLEANS: That they lack; for if their heads had any intellectual armour, they could never wear such heavy head-pieces.　　129

131   *mastiffs*, famous for their courage and tenacity.
132–3 *Foolish . . . apples.* English mastiffs were used in the pastime of bear-baiting.
132   *winking*, blindly.
134–5 *that's . . . lion*, i.e. he has no notion of his dangerous situation.

136   *sympathize with*, resemble.
137   *coming on*, attacking.

142   *stomachs*, (*a*) the bodily organ, (*b*) desire, courage.
    The scene reveals tension among the French leaders, personal animosities, slander, and backbiting. The Dauphin is concerned only with lyrical praise of his horse, the Constable with debunking the Dauphin's boasts, neither with their men, their duty, or with tactical dispositions for battle. All 'neglect' (underrate) the English whose stupidity seems so obvious.

RAMBURES: That island of England breeds very valiant creatures; their mastiffs are of unmatchable courage.

ORLEANS: Foolish curs, that run winking into the mouth of a Russian bear, and have their heads crushed like rotten apples. You may as well say that's a valiant flea that dare eat his breakfast on the lip of a lion.

CONSTABLE: Just, just; and the men do sympathize with the mastiffs in robustious and rough coming on, leaving their wits with their wives; and then give them great meals of beef and iron and steel, they will eat like wolves and fight like devils.

ORLEANS: Ay, but these English are shrewdly out of beef. 140

CONSTABLE: Then shall we find tomorrow they have only stomachs to eat and none to fight. Now is it time to arm. Come, shall we about it?

ORLEANS: It is now two o'clock; but let me see, by ten
We shall have each a hundred Englishmen.   [*Exeunt*

Chorus

1   *entertain conjecture*, imagine.

2   *poring*, eye-straining, peering. Possibly a hint of 'pouring'.

3   *wide vessel*, hollow vault.

5   *stilly*, quietly.

6–7   *That . . . watch*, so that the sentinels of both sides in the outposts could almost overhear the exchanges of their opposites.

8   *Fire answers fire*, on both sides fires arise. *paly*, (a) pale, (b) vertically barred. 'Paly' is a term in heraldry.

9   *battle*, army. *umbered*, wearing a visor or umbrere. Shadowed or stained with umber has also been suggested.

12   *accomplishing*, completing the armouring of.

13   *closing rivets up*. The helmet was riveted on to the cuirass while on the knight.

14   *note*, sound warning.

15   *toll*. An ominous word?

17   *secure*, over-confident.

18   *over-lusty*, over optimistic, over-merry.

19   *play*, i.e. gamble for prisoners. See III. vii, 79–80.

20   *tardy-gaited*, slow-footed.

23   *sacrifices*, i.e. victims to be offered to the god of war.

25–6   *gesture . . . coats*, grave expressions lining their lean, hollow cheeks, together with their war-worn coats.

ACT FOUR

Enter Chorus

CHORUS: Now entertain conjecture of a time
  When creeping murmur and the poring dark
  Fills the wide vessel of the universe.
  From camp to camp through the foul womb of night
  The hum of either army stilly sounds,
  That the fixed sentinels almost receive
  The secret whispers of each other's watch.
  Fire answers fire, and through their paly flames
  Each battle sees the other's umbered face;
  Steed threatens steed, in high and boastful neighs   10
  Piercing the night's dull ear; and from the tents
  The armourers, accomplishing the knights,
  With busy hammers closing rivets up,
  Give dreadful note of preparation,
  The country cocks do crow, the clocks do toll,
  And the third hour of drowsy morning name.
  Proud of their numbers, and secure in soul,
  The confident and over-lusty French
  Do the low-rated English play at dice;
  And chide the cripple tardy-gaited night,   20
  Who like a foul and ugly witch doth limp
  So tediously away. The poor condemned English,
  Like sacrifices, by their watchful fires
  Sit patiently, and inly ruminate
  The morning's danger; and their gesture sad
  Investing lank-lean cheeks and war-worn coats
  Presenteth them unto the gazing moon

28   *horrid*, fearful.

36   *enrounded*, surrounded.

37-8   *Nor . . . night*, neither has tiredness nor his vigil caused him to sacrifice one drop of blood from his cheeks.

38   *all-watched*, sleepless.

39   *overbears attaint*, overcomes exhaustion.

40   *semblance*, appearance. *sweet*, gracious.

43-4   *largess . . . one*, abundance of comfort, he freely bestows with his glances on all alike.

46   *as . . . define*, as far as our unworthy author can phrase it.

47   *little touch*, some small impression. *touch*, account, description.

50   *vile . . . foils*, worthless and battered swords.

51   *Right . . . ridiculous*, very badly arranged in an absurd free-for-all.

53   *Minding*, calling to mind.

The English camp at Agincourt

S.D.   Henry and Gloucester enter together and meet Bedford.
        Is Henry—meditative, reflecting, grave, jovial, high-spirited, joking, comforting, flippant, sincere, playful?

1-2   *great . . . be*. Proverbial. *King John*, II. i, 82.

So many horrid ghosts. O now, who will behold
The royal captain of this ruined band
Walking from watch to watch, from tent to tent,   30
Let him cry 'Praise and glory on his head'
For forth he goes and visits all his host,
Bids them good morrow with a modest smile,
And calls them brothers, friends, and countrymen.
Upon his royal face there is no note
How dread an army hath enrounded him;
Nor doth he dedicate one jot of colour
Unto the weary and all-watched night,
But freshly looks and overbears attaint
With cheerful semblance and sweet majesty;   40
That every wretch, pining and pale before,
Beholding him, plucks comfort from his looks.
A largess universal like the sun
His liberal eye doth give to every one,
Thawing cold fear, that mean and gentle all
Behold, as may unworthiness define,
A little touch of Harry in the night.
And so our scene must to the battle fly;
Where—O for pity—we shall much disgrace
With four or five most vile and ragged foils,   50
Right ill disposed in brawl ridiculous,
The name of Agincourt. Yet sit and see,
Minding true things by what their mock'ries be.   [*Exit*

SCENE ONE

Enter KING HENRY, BEDFORD, *and* GLOUCESTER

KING HENRY: Gloucester, 'tis true that we are in great danger,
The greater therefore should our courage be.

4–5 *There . . . out.* Proverbial: 'Nothing so bad in which there is not something of good'. *soul*, trace, spirit.

5 *observingly distil*, extract by careful search.

6–7 *For . . . husbandry.* Two proverbs are interlocked: An ill-neighbour causes an ill morrow, and early rising promotes health and wealth.

7 *husbandry*, (*a*) thrift, economy, (*b*) farming.

8 *they*, the French.

10 *dress us*, prepare ourselves.

11 *gather . . . weed*, i.e. reverse the popular belief. *weed*, profitless plant that strangles fertility.

12 *make . . . himself*, derive even from the devil good moral advice.

This speech is carefully ordered. The 'good husbandry' theme is glanced at in 'dress', prepare (a garden or plants), and 'gather honey from the weed'. The final line returns to the theme of 'goodness in evil'.

Henry uses a sequence of proverbs to give moral support—a little touch of Harry—to himself and to his nobles. This contrasts sharply with the personal disparagement and disunity shown in the proverb capping dispute of Orleans and the Constable. Is this contrast deliberate dramatic technique?

16 *likes*, pleases.

17 *Now . . . king*, i.e. Henry is also sleeping on the ground.

18–19 *love . . . example*, welcome their troubles because of an aptly applied illustration.

19–23 *so . . . legerity.* The air-like vital spirits of the body which permeated the blood conveyed messages between the mind and the body.

The image of quickening (bringing to life) is extended through revival from the dead and the discarding of grave clothes to the casting of a snake's skin.

21 *defunct and dead*, motionless and inert.

22 *drowsy grave.* Sleep as the image or counterfeit of death is a common figure in Shakespeare.

23 *legerity*, briskness, liveliness.

25 *Commend me*, give my greetings to.

31 *I . . . awhile*, I wish to meditate privately for a while.

Good morrow brother Bedford. God Almighty,
There is some soul of goodness in things evil,
Would men observingly distil it out.
For our bad neighbour makes us early stirrers,
Which is both healthful and good husbandry.
Besides they are our outward consciences,
And preachers to us all, admonishing
That we should dress us fairly for our end.   10
Thus may we gather honey from the weed,
And make a moral of the devil himself.

Enter ERPINGHAM

Good morrow, old Sir Thomas Erpingham.
A good soft pillow for that good white head
Were better than a churlish turf of France.
ERPINGHAM: Not so my liege, this lodging likes me better,
    Since I may say 'Now lie I like a king'.
KING HENRY: 'Tis good for men to love their present pains
    Upon example, so the spirit is eased.
    And when the mind is quickened, out of doubt   20
    The organs, though defunct and dead before,
    Break up their drowsy grave, and newly move
    With casted slough and fresh legerity.
    Lend me thy cloak Sir Thomas. Brothers both,
    Commend me to the princes in our camp;
    Do my good morrow to them, and anon
    Desire them all to my pavilion.
GLOUCESTER: We shall, my liege.
ERPINGHAM: Shall I attend your grace?
KING HENRY: No, my good knight.
    Go with my brothers to my lords of England.   30
    I and my bosom must debate a while,
    And then I would no other company.

37 *Discuss*, tell.
38 *popular*, of the people.
39 *gentleman of a company*, i.e. gentleman volunteer. There were many such English nobles in the Netherlands' campaigns.
40 *Trail'st ... pike?* Are you an infantry man? The pike was carried by its head while the butt trailed behind on the ground.

44 *bawcock*, fine chap. *heart of gold*, the best of fellows.
45 *imp*, child.

47 *I ... shoe*, I lick his boots, i.e. I worship and honour him.
48 *lovely bully*, grand fellow.

50 *Le Roy ... name.* Perhaps a reference to an old play *Harry of Cornwall*, or even indirectly to the Cornishman Sir Walter Ralegh whose name was variously spelt and pronounced.

55 *St Davy's day*, 1 March.

60–3 *The ... fierceness.* Some stage business is required here. Pistol's insult may rouse tension as to what Henry will do, and amusement at the situation. Does Pistol depart—swaggeringly, agitatedly, fearfully, speedily? Does Henry dismiss him peremptorily, quietly, threateningly?
62 *My ... called*, i.e. so that Henry could inform Fluellen.
63 *sorts*, agrees.

ERPINGHAM: The Lord in heaven bless thee, noble Harry.

[Exeunt all but King

KING HENRY: God-a-mercy, old heart, thou speak'st cheerfully.

Enter PISTOL

PISTOL: Qui va là?

KING HENRY: A friend.

PISTOL: Discuss unto me, art thou officer?
  Or art thou base, common, and popular?

KING HENRY: I am a gentleman of a company.

PISTOL: Trail'st thou the puissant pike?   40

KING HENRY: Even so. What are you?

PISTOL: As good a gentleman as the Emperor.

KING HENRY: Then you are a better than the King.

PISTOL: The King's a bawcock, and a heart of gold,
  A lad of life, an imp of fame;
  Of parents good, of fist most valiant.
  I kiss his dirty shoe, and from heart-string
  I love the lovely bully. What is thy name?

KING HENRY: Harry le Roy.

PISTOL: Le Roy, a Cornish name. Art thou of Cornish crew? 50

KING HENRY: No, I am a Welshman.

PISTOL: Know'st thou Fluellen?

KING HENRY: Yes.

PISTOL: Tell him I'll knock his leek about his pate
  Upon Saint Davy's day.

KING HENRY: Do not you wear your dagger in your cap that
  day, lest he knock that about yours.

PISTOL: Art thou his friend?

KING HENRY: And his kinsman too.

PISTOL: The figo for thee then!   60

KING HENRY: I thank you; God be with you.

PISTOL: My name is Pistol called.   *[Exit*

KING HENRY: It sorts well with your fierceness.

S.D.   Who enters first—Gower calling for Fluellen who then arrives or Fluellen walking briskly followed by Gower?

65   *speak lower*. The Folio has 'speake fewer'. To 'speak few' was a current expression, and the Folio reading therefore is a possible one.

65–6   *It . . . world*, it is utterly astounding that the ancient principles of military discipline are being disregarded.

67   *prerogatifes*, principles.

69   *Pompey the Great*. Pompeius Maximus (106–48 B.C.), an outstanding Roman general.

71, 72, *ceremonies, cares, forms, sobriety, modesty*. Fluellen is concerned that
   73   wars shall be conducted according to the rules laid down in military treatises.

73   *modesty*, correct conduct.

81–2   *Though . . . Welshman*. The contrast between Pistol and Fluellen is sharpened by the juxtaposition of these two incidents. Henry's praise for Fluellen is also indirectly condemnation of Pistol.

81   *out of fashion*, oddly expressed.

S.D.   The entry and speech should indicate a slower tempo and graver feelings. Do they stand, sit or lean? How are they grouped to give Henry prominence?

Act Four, Scene One

Enter FLUELLEN *and* GOWER

GOWER: Captain Fluellen.

FLUELLEN: So, in the name of Jesu Christ, speak lower. It is the greatest admiration in the universal world, when the true and aunchient prerogatifes and laws of the wars is not kept. If you would take the pains but to examine the wars of Pompey the Great, you shall find, I warrant you, that there is no tiddle taddle nor pibble pabble in Pompey's camp. I warrant you, you shall find the ceremonies of the wars, and the cares of it, and the forms of it, and the sobriety of it, and the modesty of it, to be otherwise. 73

GOWER: Why the enemy is loud, you hear him all night.

FLUELLEN: If the enemy is an ass and a fool and a prating coxcomb, is it meet, think you, that we should also, look you, be an ass and a fool and a prating coxcomb, in your own conscience now?

GOWER: I will speak lower.

FLUELLEN: I pray you and beseech you that you will.

[Exeunt Gower and Fluellen

KING HENRY: Though it appear a little out of fashion,
There is much care and valour in this Welshman. 82

Enter three soldiers, JOHN BATES, ALEXANDER COURT, *and* MICHAEL WILLIAMS

COURT: Brother John Bates, is not that the morning which breaks yonder?

BATES: I think it be. But we have no great cause to desire the approach of day.

WILLIAMS: We see yonder the beginning of the day, but I think we shall never see the end of it. Who goes there?

KING HENRY: A friend.

WILLIAMS: Under what captain serve you? 90

155

91   *Under ... Erpingham.* The cloak may have borne Erpingham's coat-of-arms.

93   *I ... estate.* Anxiety to know what is the attitude of the leaders.

94   *sand*, sand bank.

99   *element shows*, sky appears.

100–1 *conditions*, qualities.

102–4 *though ... wing*, though his feelings rise to a greater height than ours yet like ours they too sink down to earth.

102,   *higher mounted*, soar higher. *stoop*, descend. Both are terms from
103   falconry.

104–7 *Therefore ... army.* According to military textbooks a good general holds a balance between courage and fear. Lack of fear in a general was a disadvantage: 'When valour preys on reason, It eats the sword it fights with' is Enobarbus' comment on Antony (*Antony and Cleopatra*, III. xiii, 199–200).

105   *relish*, taste.

106   *possess him*, allow himself to be possessed by.

110–   *at all adventures*, at all costs.
 11

112   *my conscience*, my own true belief.
      Bates' suggestion that he and Henry share the same wish is rejected by Henry's 'higher mounted' 'affections'. Henry desires death in an honourable cause.

113–   *I ... is.* Dramatic irony.
 14

115–   *Then ... saved.* Bates introduces the immediate issue of saving life.
 16

117–   *I ... honourable.* Henry touches on loyalty to himself and the
 21   justice of his cause, pointed by the dramatic irony.

118–   *howsoever ... minds*, i.e. you say this to invite other men's
 19   opinions.

124–6 *If ... us.* Most writers on the subject supported this point of view.

KING HENRY: Under Sir Thomas Erpingham.

WILLIAMS: A good old commander and a most kind gentleman: I pray you, what thinks he of our estate?

KING HENRY: Even as men wrecked upon a sand, that look to
be washed off the next tide.

BATES: He hath not told his thought to the King?

KING HENRY: No; nor it is not meet he should. For though
I speak it to you, I think the King is but a man, as I am: the
violet smells to him as it doth to me; the element shows
to him as it doth to me; all his senses have but human conditions. His ceremonies laid by, in his nakedness he appears
but a man; and though his affections are higher mounted
than ours, yet when they stoop, they stoop with the like
wing. Therefore when he sees reason of fears, as we do, his
fears, out of doubt, be of the same relish as ours are; yet in
reason, no man should possess him with any appearance of
fear, lest he by showing it should dishearten his army.

BATES: He may show what outward courage he will; but I
believe, as cold a night as 'tis, he could wish himself in Thames
up to the neck; and so I would he were, and I by him, at all
adventures, so we were quit here.   111

KING HENRY: By my troth, I will speak my conscience of the
King: I think he would not wish himself any where but where
he is.

BATES: Then I would he were here alone; so should he be sure
to be ransomed, and a many poor men's lives saved.

KING HENRY: I dare say you love him not so ill to wish him
here alone, howsoever you speak this to feel other men's
minds; methinks I could not die any where so contented as
in the King's company, his cause being just and his quarrel
honourable.   121

WILLIAMS: That's more than we know.

BATES: Ay, or more than we should seek after; for we know
enough, if we know we are the King's subjects. If his cause be

129–
30   *at . . . day*, at the Day of Judgment.

133   *rawly*, abruptly, without protection. *die well*, die a christian death.

134–5 *charitably . . . argument*, die in love and charity when they are engaged in killing their fellow men.
      Perhaps the phrase glances at the charitable provision for widows and fatherless mentioned earlier.

137   *proportion of subjection*, rightful duties of a subject.

139   *sinfully miscarry*, die in his sins, i.e. without repentance. *imputation*, responsibility.

143   *irreconciled*, without absolution.

149   *arbitrement of swords*, trial by battle.

152   *broken . . . perjury*, false oaths, broken promises.

153   *bulwark*, shelter, protection. *gored*. Is this prompted by 'bul-wark'?

155   *native*, in their country.

156–7 *though . . . vengeance*. Direct allusion to *Psalms*, cxxxix. 9 and *Amos*, ix. 2–4.

157   *beadle*. Officer who whipped criminals.

158–9 *King's laws . . . King's quarrel*. The balance suggests apt justice.

wrong, our obedience to the King wipes the crime of it out of us. 126

WILLIAMS: But if the cause be not good, the King himself hath a heavy reckoning to make, when all those legs and arms and heads, chopped off in a battle, shall join together at the latter day and cry all 'We died at such a place'; some swearing, some crying for a surgeon, some upon their wives left poor behind 'iem, some upon the debts they owe, some upon their children rawly left. I am afeard there are few die well that die in a battle; for how can they charitably dispose of any thing, when blood is their argument? Now if these men do not die well, it will be a black matter for the king that led them to it; whom to disobey were against all proportion of subjection. 137

KING HENRY: So, if a son that is by his father sent about merchandise do sinfully miscarry upon the sea, the imputation of his wickedness, by your rule, should be imposed upon his father that sent him. Or if a servant under his master's command transporting a sum of money, be assailed by robbers and die in many irreconciled iniquities, you may call the business of the master the author of the servant's damnation. But this is not so. The king is not bound to answer the particular endings of his soldiers, the father of his son, nor the master of his servant; for they purpose not their death, when they purpose their services. Besides, there is no king, be his cause never so spotless, if it come to the arbitrement of swords, can try it out with all unspotted soldiers. Some peradventure have on them the guilt of premeditated and contrived murder; some, of beguiling virgins with the broken seals of perjury; some, making the wars their bulwark, that have before gored the gentle bosom of peace with pillage and robbery. Now if these men have defeated the law and outrun native punishment, though they can outstrip men, they have no wings to fly from God. War is his beadle, war is his vengeance; so that here men are punished for before-breach of the King's laws in now the

159–
60 *where . . . perish. Matt.* xvi. 25.

161 *unprovided*, unprepared, without making their peace with God.

163 *visited*, punished.

166 *mote*, speck of evil.

166–7 *death . . . advantage. Phil.* i. 21. For the scriptural references see Introduction, p. 21.

172–3 *'Tis . . . it.* Williams accepts Henry's argument.

178–
80 *Ay . . . wiser.* Is Williams—sceptical, humorous, realistic, unbelieving, gloomy, sarcastic, pessimistic?

182 *him.* Stressed.

182–4 *That's . . . monarch*, for a poor private person to attempt to direct his displeasure at a king is like trying to fire a deadly bullet out of a pop-gun.

    Do the three soldiers show—amusement, scorn, contempt, agreement?

187 *round*, outspoken, blunt.

192 *gage*, pledge, glove.

King's quarrel. Where they feared the death, they have borne life away; and where they would be safe, they perish. Then if they die unprovided, no more is the King guilty of their damnation than he was before guilty of those impieties for the which they are now visited. Every subject's duty is the King's, but every subject's soul is his own. Therefore should every soldier in the wars do as every sick man in his bed, wash every mote out of his conscience; and dying so, death is to him advantage; or not dying, the time was blessedly lost wherein such preparation was gained. And in him that escapes, it were not sin to think that making God so free an offer, he let him outlive that day to see his greatness and to teach others how they should prepare. 171

WILLIAMS: 'Tis certain, every man that dies ill, the ill upon his own head, the King is not to answer it.

BATES: I do not desire he should answer for me, and yet I determine to fight lustily for him.

KING HENRY: I myself heard the King say he would not be ransomed.

WILLIAMS: Ay, he said so to make us fight cheerfully; but when our throats are cut, he may be ransomed, and we ne'er the wiser. 180

KING HENRY: If I live to see it, I will never trust his word after.

WILLIAMS: You pay him then! That's a perilous shot out of an elder-gun, that a poor and a private displeasure can do against a monarch. You may as well go about to turn the sun to ice with fanning in his face with a peacock's feather. You'll never trust his word after; come, 'tis a foolish saying.

KING HENRY: Your reproof is something too round, I should be angry with you, if the time were convenient.

WILLIAMS: Let it be a quarrel between us, if you live.

KING HENRY: I embrace it. 190

WILLIAMS: How shall I know thee again?

KING HENRY: Give me any gage of thine, and I will wear it in

202   *take*, strike.

204   *Keep thy word*. An ironic back-glance at ll. 181–9.

207   *lay*, (*a*) bet, (*b*) match.
208   *crowns*, (*a*) gold coins, (*b*) heads.
209   *treason*. Those who stole silver or gold by clipping coins committed treason.

212   *careful*, anxious.

215   *Twin-born with*, inseparable from. *subject . . . breath*, at the mercy of the criticisms. *breath*, utterance, comment, criticism.
216–   *whose . . . wringing*, who has no awareness of anything beyond his
   17 own pains.
217   *wringing*, belly-ache.
218   *neglect*, forgo.
220   *ceremony*, dignities and authority.
221   *idol*, false god.

224   *rents*, gains.

my bonnet. Then, if ever thou darest acknowledge it, I will
make it my quarrel.

WILLIAMS: Here's my glove. Give me another of thine.

KING HENRY: There.

WILLIAMS: This will I also wear in my cap. If ever thou come
to me and say, after tomorrow, 'This is my glove', by this
hand I will take thee a box on the ear.

KING HENRY: If ever I live to see it, I will challenge it.   200

WILLIAMS: Thou darest as well be hanged.

KING HENRY: Well, I will do it, though I take thee in the
King's company.

WILLIAMS: Keep thy word. Fare thee well.

BATES: Be friends, you English fools, be friends; we have
French quarrels enow, if you could tell how to reckon.

KING HENRY: Indeed, the French may lay twenty French
crowns to one, they will beat us; for they bear them on their
shoulders. But it is no English treason to cut French crowns,
and tomorrow the King himself will be a clipper.   210

[*Exeunt Soldiers*

Upon the King; let us our lives, our souls,
Our debts, our careful wives,
Our children and our sins lay on the King.
We must bear all. O hard condition,
Twin-born with greatness, subject to the breath
Of every fool, whose sense no more can feel
But his own wringing. What infinite heart's-ease
Must kings neglect, that private men enjoy.
And what have kings that privates have not too,
Save ceremony, save general ceremony?   220
And what art thou, thou idol ceremony?
What kind of god art thou, that suffer'st more
Of mortal griefs than do thy worshippers?
What are thy rents, what are thy comings in?
O ceremony, show me but thy worth.

226   *What . . . adoration*, what is the real essence of the worship given to you.

227   *place . . . form*, position, rank, and formality.

232   *be sick*, i.e. from poisoned flattery.

234-5 *Think'st . . . adulation*, do you think that your burning sickness from flattery will be extinguished by the breath of flatterers proclaiming your titles?

236   *flexure*, bowing.

238   *proud dream*, illusion of greatness. See Sonnet 87.

241   *balm*, oil used to annoint a king on his coronation.

243   *intertissued*, interwoven. 'Tissue' was originally a woven cloth containing gold thread.

244   *farced . . . king*, the crowded list of titles with which a king is addressed.

245-6 *nor . . . world*, nor the proud pomp which swells up like the tides which rise high on the world's beaches.

249-   *Can . . . bread*. The thought was a common one. See *Eccles*. v. 12,
51   'The sleep of a labouring man is sweet'.

251   *distressful*, hard-earned, i.e. by the sweat of his brow. Perhaps a parallel with 'farced title' (l. 244).

252   *horrid*, fearful, terrifying. *night . . . hell*. The goddess Hecate in classical myth.

253   *lackey*, a footman who ran by a carriage.

254   *Phœbus*, sun-god who drove the chariot of the sun.

255   *Elysium*, abode of the blessed, paradise.

256   *Hyperion*, another name for the sun-god.

What is thy soul of adoration?
Art thou aught else but place, degree, and form,
Creating awe and fear in other men?
Wherein thou art less happy being feared
Than they in fearing.   230
What drink'st thou oft, instead of homage sweet,
But poisoned flattery? O be sick, great greatness,
And bid thy ceremony give thee cure.
Think'st thou the fiery fever will go out
With titles blown from adulation?
Will it give place to flexure and low bending?
Canst thou, when thou command'st the beggar's knee,
Command the health of it? No, thou proud dream,
That play'st so subtly with a king's repose.
I am a king that find thee; and I know   240
'Tis not the balm, the sceptre, and the ball,
The sword, the mace, the crown imperial,
The intertissued robe of gold and pearl,
The farced title running 'fore the king,
The throne he sits on, nor the tide of pomp
That beats upon the high shore of this world,
No, not all these, thrice-gorgeous ceremony,
Not all these, laid in bed majestical,
Can sleep so soundly as the wretched slave,
Who with a body filled and vacant mind   250
Gets him to rest, crammed with distressful bread;
Never sees horrid night, the child of hell,
But like a lackey, from the rise to set
Sweats in the eye of Phœbus, and all night
Sleeps in Elysium; next day after dawn,
Doth rise and help Hyperion to his horse,
And follows so the ever-running year,
With profitable labour to his grave:
And but for ceremony, such a wretch,

260   *Winding up*, occupying.
261   *Had ... king*, would have foremost advantage over a king.
262   *member*, sharer.
263   *wots*, knows.

265   *Whose ... advantages*, i.e. the hours spent by the king are of great
      benefit to the peasant.

266   *jealous*, anxious.

270– *O ... pardon*. For this prayer should Henry kneel, stand, clasp his
  86 hands together, raise his sword as a cross, come forward on the
      stage, turn his back to the audience, cross himself?
272–3 *The ... them*. Editors generally emend 'of' to 'if', 'lest', or 'or' and
      remove the stop after 'numbers' and render 'hearts' as 'courage'.
      But the words make good sense as they stand: 'hearts' = mind,
      understanding, intelligence, here it is loosely similar in meaning
      to 'sense of reckoning'.
273–5 *Not ... crown*. The emphatic negatives emphasize Henry's stress of
      mind that the sin of his father should not be visited on him.
275   *compassing*, usurping.
276   *I ... new*. In Westminster Abbey with his Queen.
280–1 *Who ... blood*, who pray twice daily seeking pardon for the
      guilt of murder.

282   *Two chantries*. Two religious houses for monks at Sheen and at
      Sion, Twickenham. *sad*, grave.
283   *Sing*, masses for Richard's soul. *still*, continually.

285–6 *Since ... pardon*, i.e. as my repentance and atonement come after
      all these things have happened.

Winding up days with toil and nights with sleep,   260
Had the fore-hand and vantage of a king.
The slave, a member of the country's peace,
Enjoys it; but in gross brain little wots
What watch the king keeps to maintain the peace,
Whose hours the peasant best advantages.

Enter ERPINGHAM

ERPINGHAM: My lord, your nobles, jealous of your absence,
　Seek through your camp to find you.
KING HENRY:　　　　　　　　　Good old knight,
　Collect them all together at my tent:
　I'll be before thee.
ERPINGHAM:　　　I shall do 't, my lord.   [*Exit*
KING HENRY: O God of battles, steel my soldiers' hearts,   270
　Possess them not with fear; take from them now
　The sense of reckoning of the opposed numbers
　Pluck their hearts from them. Not today, O Lord,
　O not today, think not upon the fault
　My father made in compassing the crown.
　I Richard's body have interred new,
　And on it have bestowed more contrite tears
　Than from it issued forced drops of blood.
　Five hundred poor I have in yearly pay,
　Who twice a day their withered hands hold up   280
　Toward heaven, to pardon blood. And I have built
　Two chantries, where the sad and solemn priests
　Sing still for Richard's soul. More will I do;
　Though all that I can do is nothing worth,
　Since that my penitence comes after all,
　Imploring pardon.

Enter GLOUCESTER

GLOUCESTER: My liege.

167

290   *The . . . me.* A sudden realization of how much depends on him. Is it spoken—jubilantly, with exaltation, with awe, resolutely, emphatically?

The French camp

S.D.   A noisy, vociferous entry contrasting sharply with the quiet meditative prayer of the last scene.

4–6   *Via . . . Orleans.* Editors generally have emended 'Cien' to 'Ciel', re-punctuated the lines to suit the following rendering: 'Away (over) water and land!' To which Orleans banteringly replies, 'Nothing more, not air and fire also?' And the Dauphin answers ('Yes) Heaven.' It seems clear, however, that the two speakers are referring back to the description of the horse in III. vii, 19–23, and the passage should be rendered: 'Away water and earth' Orleans: 'Nothing besides air and fire', i.e. these are the only two elements to inspire our ardour now. Orleans as earlier supports the Dauphin. 'Cien', which is the reading in the Folio, can be construed as 'Gird on' (thy sword) (Fr. ceindre).

4   *Via.* A call of encouragement to a horse (Markham).

8   *present service*, immediate action.

9   *make incision in*, spur.

10   *spin*, spurt, spray.

11   *dout*, (*a*) blind, (*b*) terrify (doubt). The 'b' was not sounded.
       superfluous courage, (*a*) overflowing blood, (*b*) abounding bravery.

17   *fair show*, splendid array.

18   *shales*, shells.

168

KING HENRY: My brother Gloucester's voice? Ay;
  I know thy errand, I will go with thee.   289
  The day, my friends, and all things stay for me.   [*Exeunt*

SCENE TWO

Enter the DAUPHIN, ORLEANS, RAMBURES,
and others

ORLEANS: The sun doth gild our armour. Up, my lords.
DAUPHIN: Montez cheval! My horse! Varlet, lacquais! Ha!
ORLEANS: O brave spirit!
DAUPHIN: Via les eaux et la terre.
ORLEANS: Rien puis l'air et le feu.
DAUPHIN: Cien cousin Orleans.

Enter CONSTABLE

  Now my lord Constable!
CONSTABLE: Hark how our steeds for present service neigh.
DAUPHIN: Mount them, and make incision in their hides,
  That their hot blood may spin in English eyes,   10
  And dout them with superfluous courage, ha!
RAMBURES: What, will you have them weep our horses' blood?
  How shall we then behold their natural tears?

Enter Messenger

MESSENGER: The English are embattled, you French peers.
CONSTABLE: To horse, you gallant princes, straight to horse.
  Do but behold yon poor and starved band,
  And your fair show shall suck away their souls,
  Leaving them but the shales and husks of men.
  There is not work enough for all our hands,
  Scarce blood enough in all their sickly veins   20

21   *curtle-axe*, cutlass.

23   *And . . . sport.* See I. ii, 112–14; III. i, 21.

24   *vapour, valour.* Is this intended as a kind of jingle to make a jocular jest? See IV. iii, 101–7 for a parallel.

25   *exceptions*, objections.

26–8   *That . . . battle.* Contrast Henry's regard for his yeomen, III. i, 25–30.

29   *hilding*, worthless.

30–1   *Though . . . speculation.* See II. iv, 57–60; I. ii, 105–10. The parallels here and those mentioned in notes to ll. 24, 26–8 between French and English mark a difference rather than a similarity. The words imply that the French look forward to avenging their defeat at Crécy.

35   *tucket sonance*, trumpet call.

36   *dare*, terrify.

37   *couch*, crouch.

39   *carrions*, skeletons. *desperate of*, despairing to save.

40   *Ill-favouredly become*, deface.

41   *ragged curtains*, tattered banners.

42   *passing*, exceedingly.

43   *Big . . . host.* Warlike spirit has vanished from their wretched men. The alliterative 'b's and perhaps a jingle on 'big' and 'beggared' emphasizes the wretchedness of the English. *Mars.* The Roman god of war.

44   *beaver*, visor, face-piece.

45–6   *The . . . hand*, the knights are motionless, like candlesticks with their spears, like match-sticks.

47   *Lob . . . hips*, hang down their heads, with flanks and hips sagging.

48   *down-roping*, oozing down.

49   *gimmalled*, double hinged ring, twin.

51   *executors*, i.e. those who dispose of a dead man's effects.

To give each naked curtle-axe a stain
That our French gallants shall today draw out,
And sheathe for lack of sport. Let us but blow on them,
The vapour of our valour will o'erturn them.
'Tis positive 'gainst all exceptions, lords,
That our superfluous lackeys and our peasants,
Who in unnecessary action swarm
About our squares of battle, were enow
To purge this field of such a hilding foe,
Though we upon this mountain's basis by   30
Took stand for idle speculation.
But that our honours must not. What's to say?
A very little let us do,
And all is done. Then let the trumpets sound
The tucket sonance and the note to mount.
For our approach shall so much dare the field
That England shall couch down in fear, and yield.

Enter GRANDPRÉ

GRANDPRÉ: Why do you stay so long, my lords of France?
  Yon island carrions, desperate of their bones,
  Ill-favouredly become the morning field.   40
  Their ragged curtains poorly are let loose,
  And our air shakes them passing scornfully.
  Big Mars seems bankrupt in their beggared host,
  And faintly through a rusty beaver peeps.
  The horsemen sit like fixed candlesticks
  With torch-staves in their hand; and their poor jades
  Lob down their heads, dropping the hides and hips,
  The gum down-roping from their pale-dead eyes,
  And in their pale dull mouths the gimmalled bit
  Lies foul with chewed grass, still and motionless.   50
  And their executors, the knavish crows,
  Fly o'er them, all impatient for their hour.

54   *the life*, to the life, the reality.
55   *In . . . lifeless*, for in real life it appears without life. The punning
     emphasizes the contempt.

57–9 *Shall . . . them?* Is the Dauphin—sarcastic, generous, inane, joking,
      serious, foolish, conceited, boastful?

60   *guidon*, pennant. Some follow the Folio and read 'guard. On'.
        'The Guidon is the first colours that any commander of horse
     can let fly in the field' (Markham, *Soldier's Accidence*, p. 416).
61   *trumpet*, trumpeter.
        The scornful description of the plight of the English serves to
     enhance their victory—which the audience of course knows in
     advance—and to sharpen the relish of witnessing the overthrow
     of the boasters.

The English camp

S.D. Entries are from different directions. Grouping should prepare for
      Henry's later speeches.

2   *The . . . battle.* The personal care sharpens the contrast with the
     French casualness. *battle*, army.

6   *bye*, be with.

8–10 *Then . . . adieu.* What form should his farewell to each one take—
      embrace, kiss, handshake, salute?

Description cannot suit itself in words
To demonstrate the life of such a battle
In life so lifeless as it shows itself.

CONSTABLE: They have said their prayers, and they stay for
death.

DAUPHIN: Shall we go send them dinners and fresh suits,
And give their fasting horses provender,
And after fight with them?

CONSTABLE: I stay but for my guidon. To the field!   60
I will the banner from a trumpet take,
And use it for my haste. Come, come, away!
The sun is high, and we outwear the day.   *[Exeunt*

SCENE THREE

Enter GLOUCESTER, BEDFORD, EXETER, ERPINGHAM,
with all his host: SALISBURY *and* WESTMORELAND

GLOUCESTER: Where is the King?

BEDFORD: The King himself is rode to view their battle.

WESTMORELAND: Of fighting men they have full three score
thousand.

EXETER: There's five to one, besides they all are fresh.

SALISBURY: God's arm strike with us, 'tis a fearful odds.
God bye you princes all; I'll to my charge.
If we no more meet till we meet in heaven,
Then joyfully, my noble Lord of Bedford,
My dear Lord Gloucester, and my good Lord Exeter,
And my kind kinsman, warriors all, adieu.   10

BEDFORD: Farewell good Salisbury, and good luck go with
thee.

EXETER: Farewell kind lord; fight valiantly today.
And yet I do thee wrong to mind thee of it,

173

23-4 *God's ... Jove.* Johnson comments, 'The King prays like a christian and swears like a heathen'. Jove was perhaps inserted later in deference to the Act (1605) against profanity in stage plays.

25 *upon my cost*, at my expense.

26 *yearns*, grieves.

28-9 *But ... alive.* This wish has been compared and contrasted with Hotspur's ill-judged search for honour, *I Henry IV*, I. iii, 201-7.

35-6 *he ... depart.* Compare God's words to Gideon, *Judges*, *vii.* 3 (Professor Maxwell privately).

35 *stomach*, courage, taste.

39 *That ... us*, who is afraid to die in fellowship with us.

40 *feast of Crispian*, 25 October. The brothers Crispinus and Crispianus were the patron saints of shoemakers. They were martyred in 287.
    Henry turns from Westmoreland to the soldiers.

42 *stand a tip-toe*, stretch himself to his full height in pride and exaltation.

For thou art framed of the firm truth of valour.

[*Exit Salisbury*

BEDFORD: He is as full of valour as of kindness;
Princely in both.

Enter the KING

WESTMORELAND: O that we now had here
But one ten thousand of those men in England
That do no work today.
KING HENRY: What's he that wishes so?
My cousin Westmoreland? No, my fair cousin:
If we are marked to die, we are enow   20
To do our country loss; and if to live,
The fewer men, the greater share of honour.
God's will, I pray thee wish not one man more.
By Jove, I am not covetous for gold,
Nor care I who doth feed upon my cost.
It yearns me not if men my garments wear;
Such outward things dwell not in my desires.
But if it be a sin to covet honour,
I am the most offending soul alive.
No faith, my coz, wish not a man from England.   30
God's peace, I would not lose so great an honour
As one man more methinks would share from me,
For the best hope I have. O, do not wish one more.
Rather proclaim it, Westmoreland, through my host,
That he which hath no stomach to this fight,
Let him depart; his passport shall be made,
And crowns for convoy put into his purse.
We would not die in that man's company
That fears his fellowship to die with us.
This day is called the feast of Crispian.   40
He that outlives this day, and comes safe home,
Will stand a tip-toe when this day is named,

44   *see . . . live.* Some editors interchange 'see' and 'live', others read
      't'old' for 'old'.

48   *And . . . day.* Added from the Quarto.
49   *yet,* some read 'yea'.
49–51 *yet . . . day.* Any response to this glimpse of humour?
50   *with advantages,* with touches of exaggeration.

56   *good man,* goodman, head of a household.

62   *vile,* humbly born.
63   *gentle his condition,* ennoble him, make him a gentleman.
         Henry later gave the right to assume a coat of arms to those
      who fought at Agincourt while denying the privilege to others.
      Henry's promise should be spoken with deliberation. What
      reactions do his listeners show during his speech—laughter,
      approval, exhilaration, patience, boredom, enthusiasm?

68   *bestow yourself,* take up your position.
69   *bravely . . . set,* well positioned in battle order.
70   *expedience,* speed.
71–5 *All . . . battle.* A demonstration of Westmoreland's readiness of
      mind. See ll. 16–18.

And rouse him at the name of Crispian.
He that shall see this day, and live old age,
Will yearly on the vigil feast his neighbours,
And say, 'Tomorrow is Saint Crispian':
Then will he strip his sleeve and show his scars,
And say 'These wounds I had on Crispin's day'.
Old men forget; yet all shall be forgot,
But he'll remember with advantages   50
What feats he did that day. Then shall our names,
Familiar in his mouth as household words,
Harry the King, Bedford and Exeter,
Warwick and Talbot, Salisbury and Gloucester,
Be in their flowing cups freshly remembered.
This story shall the good man teach his son;
And Crispin Crispian shall ne'er go by,
From this day to the ending of the world,
But we in it shall be remembered;
We few, we happy few, we band of brothers;   60
For he today that sheds his blood with me
Shall be my brother; be he ne'er so vile,
This day shall gentle his condition.
And gentlemen in England now a-bed
Shall think themselves accursed they were not here,
And hold their manhoods cheap whiles any speaks
That fought with us upon Saint Crispin's day.

Enter SALISBURY

SALISBURY: My sovereign lord, bestow yourself with speed.
  The French are bravely in their battles set,
  And will with all expedience charge on us.   70
KING HENRY: All things are ready, if our minds be so.
WESTMORELAND: Perish the man whose mind is backward
  now.

76   *five thousand men.* Probably near the actual size of Henry's army.
      So far in this scene Henry has dealt with the qualms of Westmore-
      land, asserted again his gladness at being where he is, emphasized
      the unity of his men, and received assurance of wholehearted
      support.

S.D.   The nobles do not go until after Montjoy's departure.

80   *compound*, come to terms.

83-8 *Besides . . . fester.* Is this—pity, arrogance, chivalry, contempt,
      piety, psychological warfare?

91   *achieve me*, capture me.

93-4 *The . . . him.* A version of the proverb 'Do not sell the bear's
      skin before you have caught the bear', i.e. do not promise what
      you cannot perform. The substitution of the royal 'lion' for the
      'bear' refers it to Henry himself.

96   *native*, in their own country.

100-1 *for . . . heaven*, i.e. as the sun draws up vapours from dunghills so
      shall it draw up their immortal honours to heaven. See ll. 85-8.

KING HENRY: Thou dost not wish more help from England, coz?

WESTMORELAND: God's will, my liege, would you and I alone,
Without more help, could fight this royal battle,

KING HENRY: Why now thou hast unwished five thousand men;
Which likes me better than to wish us one.
You know your places. God be with you all.

Tucket. Enter MONTJOY

MONTJOY: Once more I come to know of thee King Harry,
If for thy ransom thou wilt now compound,   80
Before thy most assured overthrow.
For certainly thou art so near the gulf,
Thou needs must be englutted. Besides, in mercy
The Constable desires thee thou wilt mind
Thy followers of repentance; that their souls
May make a peaceful and a sweet retire
From off these fields, where, wretches, their poor bodies
Must lie and fester.

KING HENRY: Who hath sent thee now?

MONTJOY: The Constable of France.

KING HENRY: I pray thee bear my former answer back.   90
Bid them achieve me and then sell my bones.
Good God, why should they mock poor fellows thus?
The man that once did sell the lion's skin
While the beast lived, was killed with hunting him.
A many of our bodies shall no doubt
Find native graves; upon the which, I trust,
Shall witness live in brass of this day's work.
And those that leave their valiant bones in France,
Dying like men, though buried in your dunghills,
They shall be famed; for there the sun shall greet them,   100
And draw their honours reeking up to heaven,

179

102-3 *Leaving ... France.* As in the previous lines Henry is replying to the Constable's message. See ll. 87–8.

104 *abounding,* (*a*) abundant, (*b*) rebounding.

105 *crasing,* ricocheting.

106 *mischief,* injury, damage.

107 *Killing ... mortality,* killing as they decay in death. Some editors interpret 'relapse of mortality' as 'deadly rebound'.

109 *for the working-day,* i.e. who are ready for deeds and not for show.

111 *painful,* laborious, toilsome.

112 *not ... host.* All the plumes on their crests are worn away.

115 *in the trim,* (*a*) in good spirits, (*b*) fashionably dressed, in contrast to 'slovenry'.

116 *poor,* poorly dressed.

117 *in fresher robes,* i.e. in Heaven. *Rev.* vi. 11; vii. 9.

119 *turn ... service,* strip from them their master's livery. Perhaps also a euphuism for 'kill them'. Elizabethan servants wore their master's livery, which was taken from them if they left his service.

127 *Thou ... more.* Is this—regretful, patronizing, arrogant, angry, threatening?

128 *I ... ransom,* i.e. to ransom the French nobles.

131-2 *Now ... away.* A formal march with drums and banners. Henry with his nobles leaves last.

Leaving their earthly parts to choke your clime,
The smell whereof shall breed a plague in France.
Mark then abounding valour in our English,
That being dead, like to the bullet's crasing,
Break out into a second course of mischief,
Killing in relapse of mortality.
Let me speak proudly. Tell the Constable
We are but warriors for the working-day.
Our gayness and our gilt are all besmirched   110
With rainy marching in the painful field.
There's not a piece of feather in our host—
Good argument, I hope, we will not fly—
And time hath worn us into slovenry.
But by the mass our hearts are in the trim;
And my poor soldiers tell me, yet ere night
They'll be in fresher robes, or they will pluck
The gay new coats o'er the French soldiers' heads,
And turn them out of service. If they do this—
As if God please, they shall—my ransom then   120
Will soon be levied. Herald, save thou thy labour;
Come thou no more for ransom, gentle herald:
They shall have none, I swear, but these my joints,
Which if they have as I will leave 'em them,
Shall yield them little, tell the Constable.

MONTJOY: I shall, King Harry. And so fare thee well.
Thou never shalt hear herald any more.   *[Exit*

KING HENRY: I fear thou 'lt once more come again for ransom.

Enter YORK

YORK: My lord, most humbly on my knee I beg
The leading of the vaward.   130

KING HENRY: Take it, brave York. Now, soldiers, march
away;
And how thou pleasest, God, dispose the day.   *[Exeunt*

King Henry V

The battlefield

S.D.   *Alarums. Excursions.* What is appropriate—trumpet calls, drumming, combats, pursuits, shouts, orders, clash of weapons?
    Do they enter from the same point or not? Has the French soldier any mark that distinguishes him as French?

4   *Qualtitie . . . me.* Some take this as the refrain of an Irish song printed in *A Handful of Pleasant Delights*, 1584. Probably a corruption of 'cailin og a stor' (young girl my darling). Others prefer to render it as 'Quality, cullion, construe me'.

7   *Signieur . . . gentleman.* Some kind of significance is intended. Perhaps 'Dew' = 'due' (of which it was an alternative spelling), i.e. that which was given to the devil who notoriously was a gentleman, and hence a blasphemous inversion of 'Dieu'. See IV. vii, 124 and *King Lear*, III. iv, 139–40, 'The prince of darkness is a gentleman'.

9   *fox*, sword. The name came from the trade mark—actually a wolf —of swords made at Passau. Any gesture?

11   *Egregious*, extraordinary.

12   *O . . . moi.* Is the French soldier standing, grovelling, kneeling, clinging to Pistol's knees?

13   *Moy . . . moys.* 'Moy' was a measure of about a bushel.

14   *rim*, diaphragm.

17, 18 *bras, brass.* Final 's' was sounded in sixteenth-century French.

19   *luxurious*, lecherous. *mountain-goat.* Is there anything in the French soldier's appearance to suggest this, or is it Pistol's odd vocabulary?

20   *Offer'st me brass*, (*a*) the metal, (*b*) perhaps 'impudence'. See *Love's Labour's Lost*, V. ii, 395, 'face of brass'.

23–4 *ask . . . name.* Has Pistol forgotten 'Signieur Dew', is this to display the Boy's knowledge of French, or has Pistol decided that he is not getting anywhere?

28   *fer, firk, ferret.* I'll give him 'fer', I'll whip him, I'll tear him to bits. *fer*, sword (French). *firk*, beat, whip. *ferret*, worry like a ferret.

SCENE FOUR

Alarum. Excursions. Enter PISTOL, *French Soldier,
and Boy*

PISTOL: Yield cur!

FRENCH SOLDIER: Je pense que vous êtes gentilhomme de
bonne qualité.

PISTOL: Qualtitie calen custure me! Art thou a gentleman?
what is thy name? Discuss.

FRENCH SOLDIER: O Seigneur Dieu!

PISTOL: O Signieur Dew should be a gentleman.
Perpend my words, O Signieur Dew, and mark.
O Signieur Dew, thou diest on point of fox,
Except, O signieur, thou do give to me   10
Egregious ransom.

FRENCH SOLDIER: O prenez miséricorde, ayez pitié de moi.

PISTOL: Moy shall not serve, I will have forty moys;
Or I will fetch thy rim out at thy throat
In drops of crimson blood.

FRENCH SOLDIER: Est-il impossible d'échapper la force de ton
bras?

PISTOL: Brass, cur?
Thou damned and luxurious mountain goat,
Offer'st me brass?   20

FRENCH SOLDIER: O pardonnez moi!

PISTOL: Say'st thou me so? Is that a ton of moys?
Come hither boy, ask me this slave in French
What is his name.

BOY: Ecoutez: comment êtes-vous appelé?

FRENCH SOLDIER: Monsieur le Fer.

BOY: He says his name is Master Fer.

PISTOL: Master Fer! I'll fer him, and firk him, and ferret him.
Discuss the same in French unto him.

36   *cuppele gorge.* Pistol's signature phrase. See II. i, 63.

39–41 O . . . *écus.* Any supplicatory gestures and tones? See l. 52.

BOY: I do not know the French for fer, and ferret, and firk.   30
PISTOL: Bid him prepare, for I will cut his throat.
FRENCH SOLDIER: Que dit-il monsieur?
BOY: Il me commande de vous dire que vous faites vous prêt, car ce soldat ici est disposé tout à cette heure de couper votre gorge.
PISTOL: Owy, cuppele gorge, permafoy,
Peasant, unless thou give me crowns, brave crowns;
Or mangled shalt thou be by this my sword.
FRENCH SOLDIER: O je vous supplie, pour l'amour de Dieu, me pardonner. Je suis gentilhomme de bonne maison: gardez ma vie, et je vous donnerai deux cents écus.   41
PISTOL: What are his words?
BOY: He prays you to save his life. He is a gentleman of a good house, and for his ransom he will give you two hundred crowns.
PISTOL: Tell him my fury shall abate, and I
The crowns will take.
FRENCH SOLDIER: Petit monsieur que dit-il?
BOY: Encore qu'il est contre son jurement de pardonner aucun prisonnier, néanmoins pour les écus que vous l'avez promis, il est content de vous donner la liberté, le franchisement.   51
FRENCH SOLDIER: Sur mes genoux je vous donne mille remercîments; et je m'estime heureux que je suis tombé entre les mains d'un chevalier, je pense le plus brave, vaillant, et très distingué seigneur d'Angleterre.
PISTOL: Expound unto me boy.
BOY: He gives you upon his knees a thousand thanks; and he esteems himself happy that he hath fallen into the hands of one, as he thinks, the most brave, valorous, and thrice-worthy signieur of England.   60
PISTOL: As I suck blood, I will some mercy show.
Follow me.

64–5   *so . . . heart*, such a loud-mouthed speech uttered by so great a coward.

66–8   *Nym . . . hanged*. No other mention that Nym was hanged.

67–8   *roaring . . . dagger*. A common feature of the morality plays was the beating of the devil with a wooden dagger to drive him from the stage. Sometimes his claw-like nails were trimmed as a further insult.

70–2   *the . . . boys*. A device to let the audience know in IV. vii, 1–5 that the Boy has been killed.

Is this scene—comic relief, satire on war, illustration of French cowardice, parody of the campaign, irony in that cowards prosper, contrast with other soldiers, captains, and nobles who fight for their king and not for themselves?

The battlefield

s.d.   Their manner of entry should indicate defeat and despair. Any further 'alarums and excursions'?

3   *confounded*, ruined.

5   *Sits . . . plumes*, i.e. the proud and gallant display of our plumes is mocked by events.

6   *Do . . . away*. Is this spoken generally or to the Constable?

7   *let's stab ourselves*. The Dauphin's suggestions are often childish.

11   *arms*. The Folio omits something here. Other suggestions are 'honour', 'harness'.

12–16 *And . . . contaminated*, i.e. anyone who will not join me in returning to fight is the most degraded and dishonourable of cowards. Bourbon stings them to action by likening them to particularly despicable cowards.

14   *pandar*, bawd, brothel keeper.

15   *gentler*, nobler, better born.

BOY: Suivez-vous le grand capitaine. [*Exeunt Pistol and French Soldier*] I did never know so full a voice issue from so empty a heart; but the saying is true, 'The empty vessel makes the greatest sound'. Bardolph and Nym had ten times more valour than this roaring devil i' th' old play, that every one may pare his nails with a wooden dagger, and they are both hanged; and so would this be, if he durst steal any thing adventurously. I must stay with the lackeys with the luggage of our camp; the French might have a good prey of us if he knew of it; for there is none to guard it but boys.   [*Exit* 72

SCENE FIVE

Enter CONSTABLE, ORLEANS, BOURBON, DAUPHIN, *and* RAMBURES

CONSTABLE: O diable!
ORLEANS: O Seigneur, le jour est perdu, tout est perdu.
DAUPHIN: Mort de ma vie, all is confounded, all.
　　Reproach and everlasting shame
　　Sits mocking in our plumes. O méchante fortune!
　　Do not run away.   [*A short alarum*
CONSTABLE:　　　Why all our ranks are broke.
DAUPHIN: O perdurable shame, let's stab ourselves.
　　Be these the wretches that we played at dice for?
ORLEANS: Is this the King we sent to for his ransom?
BOURBON: Shame and eternal shame, nothing but shame.   10
　　Let us die in arms; once more back again;
　　And he that will not follow Bourbon now,
　　Let him go hence, and with his cap in hand,
　　Like a base pandar, hold the chamber-door
　　Whilst by a slave, no gentler than my dog,
　　His fairest daughter is contaminated.

17–20 *Disorder . . . throng.* The disorder and confusion of the French emphasized by 'heaps', 'throngs' is in marked contrast with Henry's orderly control and swift decisions.

22–3 *The . . . long.* Bourbon with the courage of despair leads the others.

The battlefield

S.D. A more dignified 'alarum' than that which heralded Pistol. The entry should be carefully arranged, its order and control contrasting sharply with the preceding scene. How are the prisoners guarded and indicated—lack of weapons, hands on heads, etc.?

8 *Larding*, enriching.
9 *honour-owing*, honourable.

11 *haggled*, hacked, mangled.

15 *He.* Some prefer the Quarto 'And'. But Exeter may pause at the end of the previous line in his emotion before quoting York's words which are thus marked off from his actions.

19 *chivalry*, knightly deeds.

CONSTABLE: Disorder, that hath spoiled us, friend us now,
  Let us on heaps go offer up our lives.
ORLEANS: We are enow yet living in the field
  To smother up the English in our throngs,   20
  If any order might be thought upon.
BOURBON: The devil take order now, I'll to the throng.
  Let life be short, else shame will be too long.   [*Exeunt*

SCENE SIX

Alarums. Enter KING HENRY *and forces,* EXETER,
and others

KING HENRY: Well have we done, thrice valiant countrymen;
  But all's not done, yet keep the French the field.
EXETER: The Duke of York commends him to your majesty.
KING HENRY: Lives he good uncle? Thrice within this hour
  I saw him down; thrice up again, and fighting,
  From helmet to the spur all blood he was.
EXETER: In which array, brave soldier, doth he lie,
  Larding the plain; and by his bloody side,
  Yoke-fellow to his honour-owing wounds,
  The noble Earl of Suffolk also lies.   10
  Suffolk first died; and York all haggled over
  Comes to him, where in gore he lay insteeped,
  And takes him by the beard; kisses the gashes
  That bloodily did yawn upon his face.
  He cries aloud 'Tarry, dear cousin Suffolk,
  My soul shall thine keep company to heaven;
  Tarry, sweet soul, for mine, then fly abreast,
  As in this glorious and well-foughten field
  We kept together in our chivalry.'
  Upon these words I came and cheered him up.   20

26   *espoused to death.* To go to meet death as if to one's wedding was a particularly noble way of dying. See *King Lear*, IV. vi, 200; *Antony and Cleopatra*, IV. xiv, 100; *Measure for Measure*, III. i, 84–5.

26–7 *with . . . love.* Possibly a reminiscence of *Matt.* xxvi. 28, 'For this is my blood of the new testament'.

28   *pretty and sweet,* beautiful and gracious. Perhaps a reminiscence of the lament of David for Saul and Jonathan, 'lovely and pleasant in their lives, and in their death they were not divided', *2 Sam.* i. 23.

31–2 *all . . . tears,* all those womanly feelings of pity that I have inherited from my mother.

33   *compound,* come to terms, i.e. in the inner struggle with his feelings.

34   *issue too,* weep also.

s.d.   The trumpet must have given information about the French. Any pause for stage business while the matter is confirmed?

37–8 *Then . . . through.* Hall and Holinshed explain that Henry's men outnumbered were in a perilous position cumbered with prisoners. Are the prisoners killed on or off stage?

The noble dignified deaths of York and Suffolk which have no parallel in Shakespeare's sources are patterns of honourable and christian death in unity and loyalty, i.e. 'death is to him advantage'. Again a contrast is made with the suicidal tendencies of the Dauphin and the despair of the Constable and Orleans.

Henry's terrible decision is again a demonstration of order, control, and precise action, which contrasts with the confusion of the French.

The battlefield

s.d.   Both men are indignant.

Fluellen, knowledgeable in the rules of warfare, points out the breach of chivalry committed by the French, and Gower approves of Henry's order to kill the prisoners.

1   *Kill . . . luggage,* i.e. attack the baggage train and kill the unarmed non–combatants. *luggage.* Does Fluellen mean 'lackeys' (IV. iv, 70–2).

4   *not . . . alive.* See IV. iv, 71–2.

He smiled me in the face, raught me his hand,
And with a feeble gripe says 'Dear my lord,
Commend my service to my sovereign'.
So did he turn, and over Suffolk's neck
He threw his wounded arm, and kiss'd his lips;
And so espoused to death, with blood he sealed
A testament of noble-ending love.
The pretty and sweet manner of it forced
Those waters from me which I would have stopped,
But I had not so much of man in me,   30
And all my mother came into mine eyes
And gave me up to tears.
KING HENRY: I blame you not,
For hearing this, I must perforce compound
With mistful eyes, or they will issue too.   [*Alarum*
But hark, what new alarum is this same?
The French have reinforced their scattered men.
Then every soldier kill his prisoners.
Give the word through.   [*Exeunt*

SCENE SEVEN

Enter FLUELLEN *and* GOWER

FLUELLEN: Kill the poys and the luggage! 'Tis expressly against
the law of arms, 'tis as arrant a piece of knavery mark you
now, as can be offer't, in your conscience now, is it not?

GOWER: 'Tis certain there's not a boy left alive; and the
cowardly rascals that ran from the battle ha' done this slaughter.
Besides they have burned and carried away all that was in the
King's tent; wherefore the King most worthily hath caused
every soldier to cut his prisoner's throat. O 'tis a gallant King!

10   *Alexander the Pig.* Is this—harmless fun, contempt for Alexander, bitter sarcasm or irony?

14-15   *are . . . variations,* amount to the same thing except that the phrase is varied.

      To 'vary' a theme, here by synonyms, was a well-known rhetorical device. See III. vii, 30-1.

18-44   *I . . . Monmouth.* Fluellen attempts a 'comparison' of Henry and Alexander in rhetorical pattern: birthplaces, localities, actions. He has difficulties over the rivers, and ends with the delicious 'there is salmons in both'. There is some evidence that this relates to Alexander's belief that the Indus and the Nile were the same river because there were crocodiles in both.

27   *come after,* resembles. *indifferent well,* very well. *figures,* examples, comparisons.

32   *Cleitus.* Alexander and his close friend Cleitus quarrelled at a banquet. In a rage Alexander seized a spear and killed Cleitus.

36-7   *I . . . it.* I am working out a comparison between the two.

39   *in . . . judgments.* Fluellen's logic is topsy-turvy, but we gather that Henry is a better man than Alexander. It is the difference that is important.

40   *great-belly doublet,* heavily-stuffed, quilted doublet. Bombast was used as stuffing to give the effect of corpulence by contrast with the thin-belly doublet which was not stuffed.

41   *I . . . name.* Is Falstaff already to be forgotten? Fluellen's forgetfulness may simply be a trait of character. On the other hand Gower prompts him so that the audience knows that Fluellen means Alexander the Great and that he was born at Macedon, that

FLUELLEN: Ay, he was porn at Monmouth, Captain Gower. What call you the town's name where Alexander the Pig was born?   11

GOWER: Alexander the Great.

FLUELLEN: Why I pray you, is not pig great? The pig, or the great, or the mighty, or the huge, or the magnanimous, are all one reckonings, save the phrase is a little variations.

GOWER: I think Alexander the Great was born in Macedon; his father was called Philip of Macedon, as I take it.   17

FLUELLEN: I think it is in Macedon where Alexander is porn. I tell you captain, if you look in the maps of the 'orld, I warrant you sall find in the comparisons between Macedon and Monmouth, that the situations look you, is both alike. There is a river in Macedon and there is also moreover a river at Monmouth; it is called Wye at Monmouth: but it is out of my prains what is the name of the other river; but 'tis all one, 'tis alike as my fingers is to my fingers, and there is salmons in both. If you mark Alexander's life well, Harry of Monmouth's life is come after it indifferent well, for there is figures in all things. Alexander, God knows, and you know, in his rages, and his furies, and his wraths, and his cholers, and his moods, and his displeasures, and his indignations, and also being a little intoxicates in his prains, did in his ales and his angers, look you, kill his best friend Cleitus.   32

GOWER: Our King is not like him in that, he never killed any of his friends.

FLUELLEN: It is not well done, mark you now, to take the tales out of my mouth, ere it is made and finished. I speak but in the figures and comparisons of it: as Alexander killed his friend Cleitus, being in his ales and his cups; so also Harry Monmouth, being in his right wits and his good judgements, turned away the fat knight with the great-belly doublet; he was full of jests, and gipes, and knaveries, and mocks; I have forgot his name.

GOWER: Sir John Falstaff.   42

Fluellen's point is that Henry never killed any of his friends, and that rightly he turned away Falstaff. In this way Shakespeare can indulge Fluellen's Welsh idiom but make sure that the audience does not lose the thread.

S.D.   At first an alarum as Henry approaches, then a flourish as he arrives and the others assemble. Grouping again needs care so that Henry and his nobles, the prisoners, and Montjoy are clearly defined.
    This is the end of Bourbon's rally, IV. v.

47   *trumpet*, trumpeter.

52   *skirr*, scurry.

53   *Assyrian slings*. Perhaps *Judith*, *ix*. 7. 'The Assyrians . . . trust in shield, speare, and bow, and sling.'

57   *Here . . . liege*. For concentration and dramatic impact Shakespeare has advanced this incident by a day.

58   *His . . . be*. Anything in Montjoy's demeanour to justify this?

60   *fined*, wagered. See IV. iii, 91, 123.

61   *Com'st . . . ransom*. Is Henry—ironical, questioning, indignant, amused?

62   *charitable licence*, permission in christian charity.

64   *book*, record.

65–9   *To . . . princes*. A marked contrast with Henry's promise to those who shed their blood with him.

69   *their*. Folio has 'with'.

FLUELLEN: That is he. I'll tell you there is good men porn at
Monmouth.

GOWER: Here comes his majesty.

Alarum. Enter KING HENRY, *and forces*; WARWICK,
GLOUCESTER, EXETER, *and others*

KING HENRY: I was not angry since I came to France
Until this instant. Take a trumpet herald,
Ride thou unto the horsemen on yon hill.
If they will fight with us, bid them come down,
Or void the field; they do offend our sight.   50
If they'll do neither, we will come to them,
And make them skirr away, as swift as stones
Enforced from the old Assyrian slings.
Besides, we'll cut the throats of those we have,
And not a man of them that we shall take
Shall taste our mercy. Go and tell them so.

Enter MONTJOY

EXETER: Here comes the herald of the French, my liege.

GLOUCESTER: His eyes are humbler than they used to be.

KING HENRY: How now, what means this, herald? Know'st
thou not
That I have fined these bones of mine for ransom?   60
Com'st thou again for ransom?

MONTJOY: No great King:
I come to thee for charitable licence,
That we may wander o'er this bloody field
To book our dead, and then to bury them;
To sort our nobles from our common men.
For many of our princes—woe the while—
Lie drowned and soaked in mercenary blood.
So do our vulgar drench their peasant limbs
In blood of princes; and their wounded steeds

195

70   *Fret,* chafe. *rage,* frenzy, violence.
71   *Yerk,* kick.
72   *Killing them twice,* i.e. kicking them again with fatal blows.

74–7 *I . . . field.* Henry invites Montjoy formally to concede victory according to the rules of war.
76   *peer,* appear.

83   *grandfather,* i.e. great grandfather, Edward III.

85–6 *prave pattle,* Crécy.

89–90 *the . . . caps.* There is no other record of this 'service'. Other traditions have it that it commemorates a British victory over the Saxons in 540.
90   *Monmouth caps,* round, brimless caps with a high tapering crown.

95   *For . . . countryman.* Perhaps a glance at Queen Elizabeth I who acknowledged her Welsh descent on St David's day.

101–4 *By . . . man.* Fluellen's enthusiasm leads him to patronize Henry. He says what in fact Henry might have said to him!
     Is this reminder of Welsh deeds and Henry's ancestry—topical, irrelevant, uniting, comical?

Fret fetlock deep in gore, and with wild rage   70
Yerk out their armed heels at their dead masters,
Killing them twice. O give us leave great King,
To view the field in safety and dispose
Of their dead bodies.

KING HENRY: I tell thee truly, herald,
I know not if the day be ours or no,
For yet a many of your horsemen peer
And gallop o'er the field.

MONTJOY: The day is yours.

KING HENRY: Praised be God, and not our strength for it.
What is this castle called that stands hard by?

MONTJOY: They call it Agincourt.   80

KING HENRY: Then call we this the field of Agincourt,
Fought on the day of Crispin Crispianus.

FLUELLEN: Your grandfather of famous memory, an 't please
your majesty, and your great-uncle Edward the Plack Prince
of Wales, as I have read in the chronicles, fought a most prave
pattle here in France.

KING HENRY: They did Fluellen.   87

FLUELLEN: Your majesty says very true. If your majesties is
remembered of it, the Welshmen did good service in a garden
where leeks did grow, wearing leeks in their Monmouth caps,
which your majesty know to this hour is an honourable badge
of the service. And I do believe your majesty takes no scorn to
wear the leek upon Saint Tavy's day.

KING HENRY: I wear it for a memorable honour;
For I am Welsh, you know, good countryman.

FLUELLEN: All the water in Wye cannot wash your majesty's
Welsh plood out of your pody, I can tell you that. God pless it
and preserve it, as long as it pleases his grace, and his majesty
too!

KING HENRY: Thanks good my countryman.   100

FLUELLEN: By Jeshu, I am your majesty's countryman, I care

106   *just*, accurate.

113–   *a . . . night.* Emphatic dramatic irony.
  14
115–   *or . . . soundly.* Henry was wearing his crown.
  17

123   *sort*, rank. *quite . . . degree*, i.e. too high in rank to lower himself by
       accepting a challenge from an ordinary soldier.
124–9 *Though . . . la.* Fluellen's insistence on oath-keeping increases the
       interest and irony in Henry's predicament. Does Henry show any
       reaction, particularly to the comparison with Lucifer and Belze-
       bub?
124   *as . . . is.* Almost proverbial. See *King Lear*, III. iv, 139–40, 'The
       prince of darkness is a gentleman'.

not who know it. I will confess it to all the 'orld; I need not to
be ashamed of your majesty, praised be God, so long as your
majesty is an honest man.

Enter WILLIAMS

KING HENRY: God keep me so. Our heralds go with him.
Bring me just notice of the numbers dead
On both our parts. Call yonder fellow hither.
                          [*Exeunt Heralds with Montjoy*
EXETER: Soldier, you must come to the King.
KING HENRY: Soldier, why wear'st thou that glove in thy cap?
WILLIAMS: An 't please your majesty, 'tis the gage of one that
    I should fight withal, if he be alive.   111
KING HENRY: An Englishman?
WILLIAMS: An 't please your majesty, a rascal that swaggered
    with me last night; who if alive and ever dare to challenge this
    glove, I have sworn to take him a box o' th' ear; or if I can see
    my glove in his cap, which he swore as he was a soldier he
    would wear if alive, I will strike it out soundly.
KING HENRY: What think you Captain Fluellen, is it fit this
    soldier keep his oath?
FLUELLEN: He is a craven and a villain else, an 't please your
    majesty, in my conscience.   121
KING HENRY: It may be his enemy is a gentleman of great
    sort, quite from the answer of his degree.
FLUELLEN: Though he be as good a gentleman as the devil is,
    as Lucifer and Belzebub himself, it is necessary, look your
    grace, that he keep his vow and his oath. If he be perjured,
    see you now, his reputation is as arrant a villain and a Jacksauce
    as ever his black shoe trod upon God's ground and his earth, in
    my conscience, la !
KING HENRY: Then keep thy vow sirrah, when thou meetest
    the fellow.   131
WILLIAMS: So I will my liege, as I live.

139–   *Here . . . love.* Is this—turning the tables on Fluellen or conferring
44   an honour on him?

140–1 *when . . . helm.* The chronicles record that Henry was almost
      felled by Alençon as he went to the rescue of York.

152–3 *Pray . . . tent.* See ll. 139–40. Henry ensures that Williams and
      Fluellen will meet.

163   *mischief*, injury.
165   *touched*, easily fired, quick tempered.
      Are the nobles—anxious, amused, bewildered? Is Henry—
      playful, diplomatic, dishonest, prudent, stickler for rank,
      embarrassed?

KING HENRY: Who servest thou under?

WILLIAMS: Under Captain Gower, my liege.

FLUELLEN: Gower is a good captain, and is good knowledge and literatured in the wars.

KING HENRY: Call him hither to me, soldier.

WILLIAMS: I will, my liege.   [*Exit*

KING HENRY: Here Fluellen, wear thou this favour for me and stick it in thy cap. When Alençon and myself were down together, I plucked this glove from his helm. If any man challenge this, he is a friend to Alençon, and an enemy to our person; if thou encounter any such, apprehend him, an thou dost me love.   144

FLUELLEN: Your grace doo's me as great honours as can be desired in the hearts of his subjects. I would fain see the man that has but two legs that shall find himself aggriefed at this glove; that is all; but I would fain see it once, an please God of his grace that I might see.

KING HENRY: Know'st thou Gower?   150

FLUELLEN: He is my dear friend, an please you.

KING HENRY: Pray thee go seek him, and bring him to my tent.

FLUELLEN: I will fetch him.   [*Exit*

KING HENRY: My Lord of Warwick, and my brother Gloucester,
Follow Fluellen closely at the heels,
The glove which I have given him for a favour
May haply purchase him a box o' th' ear;
It is the soldier's; I by bargain should
Wear it myself. Follow good cousin Warwick.   160
If that the soldier strike him, as I judge
By his blunt bearing he will keep his word,
Some sudden mischief may arise of it.
For I do know Fluellen valiant,
And touched with choler, hot as gunpowder,

Before King Henry's tent

1–4   *I ... of.* Both assume that Gower is to be rewarded, but the
matter is dropped.

3   *toward you,* intended for you.

20   *contagious,* villainous, evil-spreading.

And quickly will return an injury.
Follow, and see there be no harm between them.
Go you with me, uncle of Exeter.   [*Exeunt*

SCENE EIGHT

Enter GOWER *and* WILLIAMS

WILLIAMS: I warrant it is to knight you, captain.

Enter FLUELLEN

FLUELLEN: God's will and his pleasure, captain, I beseech you
now, come apace to the king: there is more good toward you
peradventure than is in your knowledge to dream of.

WILLIAMS: Sir, know you this glove?

FLUELLEN: Know the glove? I know the glove is a glove.

WILLIAMS: I know this, and thus I challenge it.   [*Strikes him*

FLUELLEN: 'Sblood, an arrant traitor as any is in the universal
world, or in France, or in England!

GOWER: How now sir, you villain!   10

WILLIAMS: Do you think I'll be forsworn?

FLUELLEN: Stand away Captain Gower; I will give treason his
payment into plows, I warrant you.

WILLIAMS: I am no traitor.

FLUELLEN: That's a lie in thy throat. I charge you in his
majesty's name apprehend him, he's a friend of the Duke
Alençon's.

Enter WARWICK *and* GLOUCESTER

WARWICK: How now, how now, what's the matter?

FLUELLEN: My Lord of Warwick, here is—praised be God for
it—a most contagious treason come to light, look you, as you
shall desire in a summer's day. Here is his majesty.   21

22   *How . . . matter?* Dramatic irony.

31   *arrant*, utter.

33   *avouchment*, i.e. acknowledge, avow.

38   *thou . . . terms*, your remarks to me were hostile and harsh.

41   *make me satisfaction*, i.e. offer me an apology, make up for the wrong you did me.

45–50 *you . . . me.* Is Williams—surly, dignified, complaining, manly, insulting, robust, courageous, indifferent, intelligent?

Act Four, Scene Eight

Enter KING HENRY *and* EXETER

KING HENRY: How now, what's the matter?

FLUELLEN: My liege, here is a villain and a traitor, that look your grace, has struck the glove which your majesty is take out of the helmet of Alençon.

WILLIAMS: My liege, this was my glove, here is the fellow of it; and he that I gave it to in change promised to wear it in his cap. I promised to strike him, if he did. I met this man with my glove in his cap, and I have been as good as my word.   29

FLUELLEN: Your majesty hear now, saving your majesty's manhood, what an arrant, rascally, beggarly, lousy knave it is. I hope your majesty is pear me testimony and witness, and will avouchment, that this is the glove of Alençon that your majesty is give me, in your conscience now.

KING HENRY: Give me thy glove, soldier; look, here is the fellow of it.

'Twas I indeed thou promised'st to strike,
And thou hast given me most bitter terms.

FLUELLEN: And please your majesty, let his neck answer for it, if there is any martial law in the world.   40

KING HENRY: How canst thou make me satisfaction?

WILLIAMS: All offences, my lord, come from the heart; never came any from mine that might offend your majesty.

KING HENRY: It was ourself thou didst abuse.

WILLIAMS: Your majesty came not like yourself: you appeared to me but as a common man; witness the night, your garments, your lowliness; and what your highness suffered under that shape, I beseech you take it for your own fault and not mine; for had you been as I took you for, I made no offence; therefore, I beseech your highness pardon me.   50

KING HENRY: Here uncle Exeter, fill this glove with crowns,
And give it to this fellow. Keep it fellow;
And wear it for an honour in thy cap
Till I do challenge it. Give him the crowns.

57   *belly*, seat of courage.

58–60 *I . . . you.* Fluellen still remembers the dispute with Henry and his own tingling ear, and he offers advice.

61   *I . . . money.* Does Williams resent Fluellen's patronizing air, his advice, or Fluellen? Does he take the money eventually?

68   *sort*, rank.

75   *banners*, coats of arms on their own standards.

79   *dubbed*, made (with a sword).

83   *blood*, good birth and lineage.

And captain, you must needs be friends with him.

FLUELLEN: By this day and this light, the fellow has mettle enough in his belly. Hold, there is twelve pence for you, and I pray you to serve God, and keep you out of prawls and prabbles, and quarrels and dissensions, and I warrant you it is the better for you. 60

WILLIAMS: I will none of your money.

FLUELLEN: It is with a good will; I can tell you, it will serve you to mend your shoes. Come, wherefore should you be so pashful? Your shoes is not so good. 'Tis a good silling I warrant you, or I will change it.

Enter an English Herald

KING HENRY: Now herald, are the dead numbered?

HERALD: Here is the number of the slaughtered French.

KING HENRY: What prisoners of good sort are taken, uncle?

EXETER: Charles Duke of Orleans, nephew to the King,
John Duke of Bourbon, and Lord Bouciqualt. 70
Of other lords and barons, knights and squires,
Full fifteen hundred, besides common men.

KING HENRY: This note doth tell me of ten thousand French
That in the field lie slain: of princes, in this number,
And nobles bearing banners, there lie dead
One hundred twenty six; added to these,
Of knights, esquires, and gallant gentlemen,
Eight thousand and four hundred; of the which,
Five hundred were but yesterday dubbed knights.
So that in these ten thousand they have lost, 80
There are but sixteen hundred mercenaries;
The rest are princes, barons, lords, knights, squires,
And gentlemen of blood and quality.
The names of those their nobles that lie dead:
Charles Delabreth, high Constable of France,
Jacques of Chatillon, admiral of France,
The master of the cross-bows, Lord Rambures,

96–9   *Edward ... twenty.* Some would have this read by the Herald
       since 'O God ...' is indented in a fresh line in the Folio, and since
       Quartos and subsequent Folio editions insert the speech-heading
       for 'King'.

102   *plain ... play,* direct encounter and straightforward fighting.

116   *Non nobis. Psalms,* cxv. 1, formerly part of *Psalms,* cxiv.
          Procession forms to go to the village for a service of thanks-
       giving. Is it solemn and silent or accompanied by trumpets, drums,
       fifes, banners?

Great Master of France, the brave Sir Guichard Dolphin,
John Duke of Alençon, Anthony Duke of Brabant,
The brother to the Duke of Burgundy,   90
And Edward Duke of Bar; of lusty earls,
Grandpré and Roussi, Faulconbridge and Foix,
Beaumont and Marle, Vaudemont and Lestrale.
Here was a royal fellowship of death.
Where is the number of our English dead?

                               [Herald shows him another paper

Edward the Duke of York, the Earl of Suffolk,
Sir Richard Ketly, Davy Gam, esquire;
None else of name; and of all other men
But five and twenty. O God, thy arm was here;
And not to us, but to thy arm alone,   100
Ascribe we all. When, without stratagem,
But in plain shock and even play of battle,
Was ever known so great and little loss
On one part and on th' other? Take it God,
For it is none but thine.

EXETER: 'Tis wonderful.

KING HENRY: Come, go we in procession to the village.
  And be it death proclaimed through our host
  To boast of this or take that praise from God
  Which is his only.

FLUELLEN: Is it not lawful, an please your majesty, to tell how
  many is killed?   111

KING HENRY: Yes, captain; but with this acknowledgement,
  That God fought for us.

FLUELLEN: Yes, my conscience, he did us great good.

KING HENRY: Do we all holy rites;
  Let there be sung 'Non nobis' and 'Te Deum';
  The dead with charity enclosed in clay.
  And then to Calais and to England then,
  Where ne'er from France arrived more happy men.   *[Exeunt*

The Chorus describes Henry's triumphal return to London and mentions the visit of the Emperor Sigismund to bring about peace. All the campaigning and the sieges that occurred in 1417 onwards are omitted, and the play goes directly to the Treaty of Troyes, 1420.

5   *huge . . . life*, magnitude and reality.

10   *Pales*, hems, fences. *wives*, women.
11   *deep-mouthed*, roaring.
12   *whiffler*, an attendant armed with a staff who cleared the way at the head of a procession.
14   *solemnly*, with due ceremony, in state.

21   *signal*, token. *ostent*, display.

23   *quick . . . thought*, i.e. the imagination. Thought was associated with the elements of air and fire.
25   *sort*, array.

ACT FIVE

Enter Chorus

CHORUS: Vouchsafe to those that have not read the story,
That I may prompt them; and of such as have,
I humbly pray them to admit th' excuse
Of time, of numbers, and due course of things
Which cannot in their huge and proper life
Be here presented. Now we bear the king
Toward Calais. Grant him there; there seen,
Heave him away upon your winged thoughts
Athwart the sea. Behold the English beach
Pales in the flood with men, with wives, and boys,   10
Whose shouts and claps out-voice the deep-mouthed sea,
Which like a mighty whiffler 'fore the King
Seems to prepare his way. So let him land,
And solemnly see him set on to London.
So swift a pace hath thought that even now
You may imagine him upon Blackheath;
Where that his lords desire him to have borne
His bruised helmet and his bended sword
Before him through the city; he forbids it,
Being free from vainness and self-glorious pride;   20
Giving full trophy, signal, and ostent
Quite from himself to God. But now behold,
In the quick forge and working-house of thought,
How London doth pour out her citizens.
The mayor and all his brethren in best sort,
Like to the senators of th' antique Rome,
With the plebeians swarming at their heels,

29   *As . . . likelihood*, as by a humbler possibility yet one dear to our
hearts.

30   *the . . . Empress.* An allusion to the Earl of Essex who left London
on 27 March, 1599, for Ireland with an army to suppress Tyrone's
rebellion.

       Dover Wilson notes the 'skill and caution' of this compliment;
'after the reference to Cæsar to call Elizabeth "Empress" puts
Essex neatly in his place'.

32   *broached*, pierced, spitted.

36–7   *As . . . home*, so far the French are so occupied in mourning their
defeat that Henry has no reason for leaving England.

38   *The . . . France*, the Holy Roman Emperor Sigismund visited
England in May 1416.

42–3   *played The interim*, enacted the lapse of time.

44   *brook abridgement*, put up with this (*a*) short entertainment (*b*)
shortening of time. *advance*, (*a*) open, (*b*) move forward.

The English camp

S.D.   The device of continued conversation has the effect of implying a
depth to the play, of linking it up with the larger life of the army
which is not presented.

       Fluellen is armed with a cudgel and supplied with leeks.

3–4   *There . . . things.* See IV. vii, 27–8.

5   *scauld*, scabby, scurvy.

9   *breed no contention*, raise a quarrel.

Go forth and fetch their conquering Cæsar in.
As by a lower but loving likelihood,
Were now the general of our gracious Empress,   30
As in good time he may, from Ireland coming,
Bringing rebellion broached on his sword,
How many would the peaceful city quit
To welcome him! Much more, and much more cause,
Did they this Harry. Now in London place him.
As yet the lamentation of the French
Invites the King of England's stay at home;
The Emperor's coming in behalf of France,
To order peace between them; and omit
All the occurrences, whatever chanced,   40
Till Harry's back-return again to France.
There must we bring him; and myself have played
The interim, by remembering you 'tis past.
Then brook abridgement, and your eyes advance,
After your thoughts, straight back again to France.   [*Exit*

SCENE ONE

Enter FLUELLEN *and* GOWER

GOWER: Nay, that's right. But why wear you your leek today?
Saint Davy's day is past.

FLUELLEN: There is occasions and causes why and wherefore in
all things. I will tell you, asse my friend, Captain Gower. The
rascally, scauld, beggarly, lousy, pragging knave, Pistol, which
you and yourself and all the world know to be no petter than a
fellow, look you now, of no merits, he is come to me and
prings me pread and salt yesterday, look you, and bid me eat
my leek. It was in a place where I could not breed no contention
with him; but I will be so bold as to wear it in my cap till I see

213

11–12 *a . . . desires*, a piece of my mind.

13 *swelling . . . turkey-cock*. Pistol is perhaps decked out in plumes and silks the proceeds of the ransom of M. le Fer and of his own sutler-ship. *swelling*, i.e. the wattles swollen and the tail feathers spread.

17 *Bedlam*, mad. A word corrupted from Bethlehem, a London Hospital for mentally afflicted. *Trojan*, knave.

18 *fold . . . web*, kill you. *Parca's*. In classical myth the Parcæ were the three Fates who wove the web of each man's destiny. When the pattern was completed, the thread was cut and the man's life ended.

21, 23 *desires . . . petitions, affections . . . disgestions*. Fluellen varies his terms again. See IV. vii, 13–15. Compare IV. i, 71–3; IV. vii, 28–32.

23 *affections*, inclinations.

25 *Cadwallader*. The last British king.

26–50 *There . . . all*. How are the cudgelling and eating of the leek arranged—Pistol upright, kneeling, cringing, running away? Other business is indicated in ll. 35, 42–3, 47–8, 52.

32 *mountain-squire*, owner of worthless land.

32–3 *squire . . . degree*, (*a*) squire of the basest rank, (*b*) title of a medieval romantic poem.
   Fluellen contrasts 'low' with 'mountain', and quibbles on the title of the poem.

35 *astonished*, beaten him into submission, cowed.

38 *green*, raw.

41 *ambiguities*, uncertainties.

42–3 *By . . . swear*. What causes Pistol to change his tone?

him once again, and then I will tell him a little piece of my
desires. 12

Enter PISTOL

GOWER: Why here he comes, swelling like a turkey-cock.

FLUELLEN: 'Tis no matter for his swellings nor his turkey-
cocks. God pless you, Aunchient Pistol; you scurvy, lousy
knave, God pless you.

PISTOL: Ha, art thou Bedlam? Dost thou thirst, base Trojan,
To have me fold up Parca's fatal web?
Hence; I am qualmish at the smell of leek. 19

FLUELLEN: I peseech you heartily, scurvy, lousy knave, at my
desires, and my requests, and my petitions, to eat, look you,
this leek; because, look you, you do not love it, nor your
affections and your appetites and your disgestions doo's not
agree with it, I would desire you to eat it.

PISTOL: Not for Cadwallader and all his goats.

FLUELLEN: There is one goat for you. [*Strikes him.*] Will you be
so good, scauld knave, as eat it?

PISTOL: Base Trojan, thou shalt die. 28

FLUELLEN: You say very true, scauld knave, when God's will is.
I will desire you to live in the mean time, and eat your victuals.
Come, there is sauce for it. [*Strikes him.*] You called me
yesterday mountain-squire, but I will make you today a squire
of low degree. I pray you fall to, if you can mock a leek, you
can eat a leek.

GOWER: Enough captain, you have astonished him.

FLUELLEN: I say, I will make him eat some part of my leek, or
I will peat his pate four days. Bite I pray you, it is good for
your green wound and your ploody coxcomb.

PISTOL: Must I bite? 39

FLUELLEN: Yes certainly, and out of doubt and out of question
too, and ambiguities.

PISTOL: By this leek, I will most horribly revenge—
I eat and eat, I swear.

44   *sauce*, i.e. cudgel.

51   *Good*, very well, all right.
52   *groat*, fourpenny piece.

57   *earnest*, pledge.

62   *counterfeit*, sham.

64   *respect*, reason.
64–5   *predeceased valour*. See IV. vii, 88–93.
66   *gleeking*, mocking. *galling*, jeering.

70   *condition*, disposition, attitude.

71   *Doth . . . now*. Pistol's bluster turns to whining as he blames
        Fortune for his troubles. *huswife*, hussy.
72   *my Doll*. Pistol was married to Nell Quickly not Doll Tearsheet
        whom he mentioned as 'i' the spital' (II. i, 68–71).
73   *malady of France*, venereal disease.
74   *rendezvous*, home, haunt, lodging.
76   *bawd*, brothel-keeper.

FLUELLEN: Eat I pray you, will you have some more sauce to your leek? There is not enough leek to swear by.

PISTOL: Quiet thy cudgel, thou dost see I eat.

FLUELLEN: Much good do you scauld knave, heartily. Nay, pray you throw none away, the skin is good for your broken coxcomb. When you take occasions to see leeks hereafter, I pray you mock at 'em; that is all.   50

PISTOL: Good.

FLUELLEN: Ay, leeks is good. Hold you, there is a groat to heal your pate.

PISTOL: Me a groat?

FLUELLEN: Yes verily, and in truth you shall take it, or I have another leek in my pocket, which you shall eat.

PISTOL: I take thy groat in earnest of revenge.

FLUELLEN: If I owe you any thing, I will pay you in cudgels; you shall be a woodmonger, and buy nothing of me but cudgels. God bye you, and keep you, and heal your pate. [Exit

PISTOL: All hell shall stir for this.   61

GOWER: Go, go; you are a counterfeit cowardly knave. Will you mock at an ancient tradition, begun upon an honourable respect, and worn as a memorable trophy of predeceased valour, and dare not avouch in your deeds any of your words? I have seen you gleeking and galling at this gentleman twice or thrice. You thought, because he could not speak English in the native garb, he could not therefore handle an English cudgel; you find it otherwise; and henceforth let a Welsh correction teach you a good English condition. Fare ye well.   70
                                                            [Exit

PISTOL: Doth Fortune play the huswife with me now?
News have I that my Doll is dead i' th' spital
Of malady of France;
And there my rendezvous is quite cut off.
Old I do wax, and from my weary limbs
Honour is cudgelled. Well, bawd I'll turn,

77   *And . . . hand*, with a side-line in pocket picking and purse slitting.

78   *steal*, i.e. desert from the army.

79–80 *And . . . wars*, i.e. as a beggar wearing plasters which he claims
      cover wounds received at Agincourt.
          How does Pistol depart—slinking, stealthily, furtively, droop-
      ing, with a nod and wink, cock-a-hoop, with a cunning leer?

The palace at Troyes

s.d.   Full ceremonial entries preceded by fanfares. Two thrones are
        required—should they be placed side by side or opposite each
        other? Should Burgundy have a throne?

1   *Peace . . . met*, peace, for which we are met, be to this meeting.
       This solemn blessing by Henry before any greetings are exchanged
       gives the scene its key.
           The greetings and salutations require a pattern of gesture and
       movement.

7   *Burgundy*. The young Duke of Burgundy arranged the meeting
       after his father was murdered.

16   *bent*, (*a*) glance, (*b*) line of fire.

17   *balls*, (*a*) cannon balls, (*b*) eye-balls. *basilisks*, (*a*) brass cannon,
       (*b*) cockatrices. Legendary reptiles hatched by a snake from a
       cock's egg. Their glance and breath were fatal. See III. i, 8–11.

19   *quality*, power, nature.

And something lean to cutpurse of quick hand.
To England will I steal, and there I'll steal.
And patches will I get unto these cudgelled scars,
And swear I got them in the Gallia wars.   [*Exit* 80

SCENE TWO

Enter, at one door, KING HENRY, EXETER, BEDFORD, GLOU-
CESTER, WARWICK, WESTMORELAND, *and other Lords; at
another, the* FRENCH KING, QUEEN ISABEL, *the* PRINCESS
KATHARINE, ALICE, *and other Ladies; the* DUKE OF BUR-
GUNDY, *and his train*

KING HENRY: Peace to this meeting, wherefore we are met.
  Unto our brother France, and to our sister,
  Health and fair time of day; joy and good wishes
  To our most fair and princely cousin Katharine;
  And as a branch and member of this royalty,
  By whom this great assembly is contrived,
  We do salute you, Duke of Burgundy;
  And princes French, and peers, health to you all.
FRENCH KING: Right joyous are we to behold your face,
  Most worthy brother England, fairly met.   10
  So are you, princes English, every one.
QUEEN ISABEL: So happy be the issue, brother England,
  Of this good day, and of this gracious meeting,
  As we are now glad to behold your eyes;
  Your eyes which hitherto have borne in them
  Against the French, that met them in their bent,
  The fatal balls of murdering basilisks.
  The venom of such looks we fairly hope
  Have lost their quality, and that this day

20 *griefs*, injuries, wrongs.

23 *on*, on terms of.

27 *bar*, judgment place.

31 *congreeted*, exchanged greetings. *let . . . me*, let me not lose your favour.

33 *rub*, obstacle.

37 *put up*, raise.
38 *chased*. See I. ii, 265–6.
39 *all . . . heaps*, all the produce of her farms rots the more because of its abundance.
40 *it*, its.
41 *Her . . . heart*, Psalms, civ. 15, 'wine that maketh glad the heart of man'.
42 *even-pleached*, evenly layered.
      Burgundy stresses the lack of order in France.
44 *fallow leas*, unploughed fields.
45 *darnel*, rye-grass. *rank*, overgrown.
46 *coulter*, the knife at the front of the ploughshare. Here the plough-share itself.

51 *Conceives by idleness*. Idleness proverbially begets vices. *nothing teems*, produces nothing.
52 *kexes*. Plants with hollow stems, alexanders, cow-parsley, etc. *burs*, burdocks.

Shall change all griefs and quarrels into love.   20
KING HENRY: To cry amen to that, thus we appear.
QUEEN ISABEL: You English princes all, I do salute you.
BURGUNDY: My duty to you both, on equal love.
  Great Kings of France and England; that I have laboured
  With all my wits, my pains, and strong endeavours
  To bring your most imperial majesties
  Unto this bar and royal interview,
  Your mightiness on both parts best can witness.
  Since then my office hath so far prevailed
  That, face to face, and royal eye to eye,   30
  You have congreeted; let it not disgrace me,
  If I demand before this royal view,
  What rub or what impediment there is,
  Why that the naked, poor, and mangled peace,
  Dear nurse of arts, plenties, and joyful births,
  Should not in this best garden of the world
  Our fertile France, put up her lovely visage?
  Alas, she hath from France too long been chased,
  And all her husbandry doth lie on heaps,
  Corrupting in it own fertility.   40
  Her vine, the merry cheerer of the heart,
  Unpruned dies; her hedges even-pleached,
  Like prisoners wildly overgrown with hair,
  Put forth disordered twigs; her fallow leas
  The darnel, hemlock, and rank fumitory
  Doth root upon, while that the coulter rusts
  That should deracinate such savagery.
  The even mead, that erst brought sweetly forth
  The freckled cowslip, burnet, and green clover,
  Wanting the scythe, all uncorrected, rank,   50
  Conceives by idleness and nothing teems
  But hateful docks, rough thistles, kexes, burs,
  Losing both beauty and utility.

54–5   *And . . . wildness.* A summary of ll. 41–53.

55   *Defective . . . natures,* untrained by the husbandman's art.

56   *houses,* households.

58   *sciences,* knowledge, arts.

60   *That . . . blood,* whose thoughts are only of bloodshed. See IV. i, 134–5.

61   *diffused,* disordered.

63   *reduce,* lead back. *favour,* appearance.

65   *let,* hindrance.

66   *inconveniences,* misfortunes.

68   *would,* desire.

72   *tenours,* general trends.

77   *cursitory,* cursory. The Folio has 'curselarie'.

78   *articles,* terms.

79   *presently,* immediately.

81–2   *we . . . answer,* we will promptly issue our considered and final answer.

82   *peremptory,* decisive.
        Does this speech indicate mental weakness in the French King?

And as our vineyards, fallows, meads, and hedges,
Defective in their natures, grow to wildness,
Even so our houses, and ourselves, and children
Have lost, or do not learn for want of time,
The sciences that should become our country;
But grow like savages, as soldiers will
That nothing do but meditate on blood,   60
To swearing and stern looks, diffused attire,
And every thing that seems unnatural.
Which to reduce into our former favour
You are assembled; and my speech entreats
That I may know the let, why gentle Peace
Should not expel these inconveniences
And bless us with her former qualities.

KING HENRY: If, Duke of Burgundy, you would the peace,
   Whose want gives growth to th' imperfections
   Which you have cited, you must buy that peace   70
   With full accord to all our just demands;
   Whose tenours and particular effects
   You have enscheduled briefly in your hands.

BURGUNDY: The King hath heard them; to the which as yet
   There is no answer made.

KING HENRY: Well then the peace,
   Which you before so urged, lies in his answer.

FRENCH KING: I have but with a cursitory eye
   O'erglanced the articles. Pleaseth your grace
   To appoint some of your council presently
   To sit with us once more, with better heed   80
   To re-survey them, we will suddenly
   Pass our accept and peremptory answer.

KING HENRY: Brother we shall. Go, uncle Exeter,
   And brother Clarence, and you, brother Gloucester,
   Warwick and Huntingdon, go with the King;
   And take with you free power to ratify,

90   *consign*, sign together.

94   *When . . . on*, when terms pressed in too precise detail are insisted on. Queen Isabella did in fact invite Burgundy to arrange the meeting.
96   *capital*, chief.

98–9 *Fair . . . fair*. Is Henry—embarrassed, awkward, at a loss?

106 *brokenly . . . tongue*, i.e. in broken English.

108 *like you*. Henry is quick to turn the meanings of words to his own advantage.

Augment, or alter, as your wisdom best
Shall see advantageable for our dignity,
Any thing in or out of our demands,
And we'll consign thereto. Will you, fair sister,   90
Go with the princes, or stay here with us?

QUEEN ISABEL: Our gracious brother, I will go with them.
Haply a woman's voice may do some good,
When articles too nicely urged be stood on.

KING HENRY: Yet leave our cousin Katharine here with us;
She is our capital demand, comprised
Within the fore-rank of our articles.

QUEEN ISABEL: She hath good leave.
                              [*Exeunt all except Henry, Katharine, and Alice*

KING HENRY: Fair Katharine, and most
      fair,
Will you vouchsafe to teach a soldier terms
Such as will enter at a lady's ear,   100
And plead his love-suit to her gentle heart?

KATHARINE: Your majesty shall mock at me; I cannot speak
your England.

KING HENRY: O fair Katharine, if you will love me soundly
with your French heart, I will be glad to hear you confess it
brokenly with your English tongue. Do you like me, Kate?

KATHARINE: Pardonnez-moi, I cannot tell wat is 'like me'.

KING HENRY: An angel is like you Kate, and you are like an
angel.

KATHARINE: Que dit-il? Que je suis semblable à les anges?   110

ALICE: Oui, vraiment, sauf votre grace, ainsi dit-il.

KING HENRY: I said so, dear Katharine, and I must not blush
to affirm it.

KATHARINE: O bon Dieu, les langues des hommes sont pleines
de tromperies.

KING HENRY: What says she, fair one? That the tongues of
men are full of deceits?

118– *dat . . . princess*, that is what the Princess says. Alice is perhaps
19 alarmed lest she herself should be held responsible for the remark.

120 *The . . . Englishwoman*, i.e. because she rejects flattery from men.

124 *sold . . . crown*, i.e. that I have no courtly graces but merely the
manners of a peasant.

124–5 *mince it*, speak in affected love language.

126 *wear . . . suit*, exhaust my pleading.

127 *clap*, shake.

131 *undid me*, finished me off, floored me.

132 *measure*, rhythm and rhyme.

133 *strength in measure*, ability in dancing. Some Elizabethan dances
required strength of body and agility.

134–5 *vaulting . . . back*. A considerable feat. See *I Henry IV*, IV. i, 104–10.

136 *leap into*, win.

138 *lay on*, strike heavily. *jack-an-apes*, *never off*, ride on my horse as
tightly as a monkey and never be thrown.

139 *look greenly*, look sheepishly, simper.

139–40 *gasp . . . eloquence*, gulp out my speeches breathless with emotion.

140 *cunning in protestation*, skill in vowing how much I love you.

141 *urged*, compelled.

143 *sun-burning*, even sunburning. A sun-burnt face was considered
unbecoming.

144 *let . . . cook*, see me in a favourable light, present me attractively.

146–7 *but . . . too*. Throughout this speech there are changes of pace and
occasional softening of tones from otherwise outspoken bluntness.

148 *uncoined*, (*a*) pure, original, (*b*) not in circulation from one woman
to another (Dover Wilson).

150 *of infinite tongue*, overfluent, glib.

151–2 *do . . . again*. The suggestion is that their verses contain feigned
love. See *A Midsummer Night's Dream*, I. i, 31, 'With feigning
voice, verses of feigning love'. A play on the saying 'Neither
rhyme nor reason'.

ALICE: Oui, dat de tongues of de mans is be full of deceits; dat is de Princess.   119

KING HENRY: The Princess is the better Englishwoman. I' faith Kate, my wooing is fit for thy understanding. I am glad thou canst speak no better English, for if thou couldst, thou wouldst find me such a plain king that thou wouldst think I had sold my farm to buy my crown. I know no ways to mince it in love, but directly to say 'I love you'; then if you urge me farther than to say 'do you in faith?' I wear out my suit. Give me your answer, i' faith do; and so clap hands and a bargain. How say you, lady?

KATHARINE: Sauf votre honneur, me understand well.   129

KING HENRY: Marry, if you would put me to verses or to dance for your sake, Kate, why, you undid me; for the one, I have neither words nor measure, and for the other, I have no strength in measure, yet a reasonable measure in strength. If I could win a lady at leap-frog, or by vaulting into my saddle with my armour on my back, under the correction of bragging be it spoken, I should quickly leap into a wife. Or if I might buffet for my love, or bound my horse for her favours, I could lay on like a butcher, and sit like a jack-an-apes, never off. But, before God Kate, I cannot look greenly nor gasp out my eloquence, nor I have no cunning in protestation; only downright oaths, which I never use till urged, nor never break for urging. If thou canst love a fellow of this temper, Kate, whose face is not worth sun-burning, that never looks in his glass for love of any thing he sees there, let thine eye be thy cook. I speak to thee plain soldier. If thou canst love me for this, take me; if not, to say to thee that I shall die, is true; but for thy love, by the Lord, no; yet I love thee too. And while thou liv'st, dear Kate, take a fellow of plain and uncoined constancy; for he perforce must do thee right, because he hath not the gift to woo in other places; for these fellows of infinite tongue, that can rhyme themselves into ladies' favours, they do always

152   *prater*, idle chatterer.

153   *a . . . ballad*, rhyming produces mere ballads. Ballads were very popular but in general were regarded with contempt by the educated courtiers.

155   *wax*, grow.

163–6   *No . . . mine*. Again Henry's nimbleness in turning words to his advantage in debate.

171–4   *Je . . . mienne*. Does Kate preserve a straight face or does she laugh?

180   *truly-falsely*, sincerely but haltingly, in good faith but in bad grammar.

181   *at one*, of a kind, alike.

184–5   **Can . . . them**. Should Kate move to prevent Henry asking Alice?

reason themselves out again. What! A speaker is but a prater;
a rhyme is but a ballad. A good leg will fall; a straight back will
stoop; a black beard will turn white; a curled pate will grow
bald; a fair face will wither; a full eye will wax hollow; but a
good heart, Kate, is the sun and the moon, or rather the sun
and not the moon; for it shines bright and never changes, but
keeps his course truly. If thou would have such a one, take me;
and take me, take a soldier; take a soldier, take a king. And
what sayest thou then to my love? Speak my fair, and fairly,
I pray thee.   161

KATHARINE: Is it possible dat I sould love de enemy of France?

KING HENRY: No; it is not possible you should love the enemy
of France, Kate; but in loving me, you should love the friend
of France; for I love France so well that I will not part with a
village of it; I will have it all mine. And Kate, when France is
mine and I am yours, then yours is France and you are mine?

KATHARINE: I cannot tell wat is dat.   168

KING HENRY: No, Kate? I will tell thee in French, which I am
sure will hang upon my tongue like a new-married wife about
her husband's neck, hardly to be shook off. Je quand sur le
possession de France, et quand vous avez le possession de moi,
—let me see, what then? Saint Denis be my speed—donc votre
est France, et vous êtes mienne. It is as easy for me, Kate, to
conquer the kingdom as to speak so much more French. I shall
never move thee in French, unless it be to laugh at me.

KATHARINE: Sauf votre honneur, le français que vous parlez, il
est meilleur que l'anglais lequel je parle.   178

KING HENRY: No faith is 't not, Kate; but thy speaking of my
tongue, and I thine, most truly-falsely, must needs be granted
to be much at one. But Kate, dost thou understand thus much
English, canst thou love me?

KATHARINE: I cannot tell.

KING HENRY: Can any of your neighbours tell, Kate? I'll ask
them. Come, I know thou lovest me; and at night, when you

191   *with scambling*, in this stumbling fashion, i.e. not in courtly fashion but with soldierly roughness.

192–8 *Shall . . . know.* Dramatic irony in that the audience knows what happened to Henry VI.

195   *Constantinople . . . beard.* It was the earnest desire of christian kings to capture Constantinople, the former centre of the Eastern Church, from the Turks.

208–9 *untempering . . . visage*, my face's inability to soften a lady's heart.
209   *beshrew*, confound.

210   *civil wars*, i.e. against Richard II.

211   *aspect*, appearance, look.

214   *ill layer up*, i.e. crumpler up (clothes), wrinkler. *spoil*, injury, harm.

216   *wear*, possess.
217– *Put . . . blushes.* Any gesture or movement?
   18

come into your closet, you'll question this gentlewoman about me; and I know, Kate, you will to her dispraise those parts in me that you love with your heart. But good Kate, mock me mercifully, the rather, gentle Princess, because I love thee cruelly. If ever thou beest mine, Kate, as I have a saving faith within me tells me thou shalt, I get thee with scambling, and thou must therefore needs prove a good soldier-breeder. Shall not thou and I, between Saint Denis and Saint George, compound a boy, half French half English, that shall go to Constantinople and take the Turk by the beard? Shall we not? What sayest thou, my fair flower-de-luce?

KATHARINE: I do not know dat.

KING HENRY: No; 'tis hereafter to know, but now to promise. Do but now promise, Kate, you will endeavour for your French part of such a boy; and for my English moiety take the word of a king and a bachelor. How answer you, la plus belle Katharine du monde, mon très cher et divin déesse? 202

KATHARINE: Your majestee ave fausse French enough to deceive de most sage demoiselle dat is en France.

KING HENRY: Now fie upon my false French! By mine honour in true English, I love thee Kate; by which honour I dare not swear thou lovest me; yet my blood begins to flatter me that thou dost, notwithstanding the poor and untempering effect of my visage. Now beshrew my father's ambition, he was thinking of civil wars when he got me; therefore was I created with a stubborn outside, with an aspect of iron, that when I come to woo ladies, I fright them. But in faith Kate, the elder I wax, the better I shall appear; my comfort is, that old age, that ill layer up of beauty, can do no more spoil upon my face. Thou hast me, if thou hast me, at the worst; and thou shalt wear me, if thou wear me, better and better; and therefore tell me, most fair Katharine, will you have me? Put off your maiden blushes, avouch the thoughts of your heart with the looks of an empress, take me by the hand and say 'Harry of

224   *fellow . . . king*, i.e. the best king.
224-5 *best . . . fellows.* (*a*) Perhaps a glance at his 'fellowship' with his
       men. (*b*) Part of the proverb, 'The king of good fellows is
       appointed for the queen of "beggars" ' (the French were suing for
       peace). *good fellows*, boon companions.
225-7 *Come . . . English.* This series of puns shows Henry's high spirits.
225   *broken music*, music arranged in parts.
227   *break*, open, reveal.

239   *Then . . . lips.* Any action?

244   *Anglish.* Perhaps Alice's pronunciation.

250   *nice . . . kings*, little trivial conventions give way to kings.
251   *list*, limitations, barriers.

253   *follows our places*, is permitted to royalty.

England, I am thine'. Which word thou shalt no sooner bless
mine ear withal, but I will tell thee aloud 'England is thine,
Ireland is thine, France is thine, and Henry Plantagenet is
thine'; who, though I speak it before his face, if he be not
fellow with the best king, thou shalt find the best king of good
fellows. Come, your answer in broken music; for thy voice is
music, and thy English broken. Therefore queen of all,
Katharine, break thy mind to me in broken English; wilt thou
have me?

KATHARINE: Dat is as it sall please de Roi mon père.

KING HENRY: Nay, it will please him well, Kate; it shall please
him, Kate.   231

KATHARINE: Den it sall also content me.

KING HENRY: Upon that I kiss your hand, and I call you my
queen.

KATHARINE: Laissez mon seigneur, laissez, laissez; ma foi, je ne
veux point que vous abaissiez votre grandeur en baisant la
main d'une de votre seigneurie indigne serviteur; excusez-moi,
je vous supplie, mon très-puissant seigneur.

KING HENRY: Then I will kiss your lips, Kate.

KATHARINE: Les dames et demoiselles pour être baisées devant
leur noces, il n'est pas la coutume de France.   241

KING HENRY: Madam my interpreter, what says she?

ALICE: Dat it is not be de fashion pour les ladies of France,—
I cannot tell wat is baiser en Anglish.

KING HENRY: To kiss.

ALICE: Your majesty entendre bettre que moi.

KING HENRY: It is not a fashion for the maids in France to kiss
before they are married, would she say?

ALICE: Oui, vraiment.   249

KING HENRY: O Kate, nice customs curtsy to great kings.
Dear Kate, you and I cannot be confined within the weak list
of a country's fashion; we are the makers of manners, Kate;
and the liberty that follows our places stops the mouth of all

255-6 *therefore . . . yielding*. What kind of a kiss is appropriate?
256   *You . . . lips*. Henry shows—surprise, awe, wonder, playfulness?

259   *general . . . monarchs*, request made entirely by kings.
       Commentators have found Henry's wooing—rough, barbarous, disgusting, dignified, manly, political, popular with ladies, brilliant?
       Katharine they find—deceitful, modest, indelicate, charming, tactful, discreet, subtle?
261-2 *My . . . English*. Henry is holding Kate in his arms.

266   *condition*, nature, temperament.
267   *smooth*, insinuating, bland, easy.
268-9 *I . . . likeness*, i.e. I cannot persuade her to confess openly her love.

271-5 *If . . . self*. Editors condemn Burgundy for indelicacy and refer to *Romeo and Juliet*, II. i, 24-6. In any case Burgundy's humour seems strained and forced.
273   *naked and blind*, i.e. Cupid.

277-8 *Yet . . . enforces*. Yet they close their eyes and yield because love is passionate and urges them.

282   *consent winking*, agree to close her eyes and so provide her with an excuse.
284-5 *well . . . kept*, well-bred and delicately reared.
284   *summered*, pastured, matured.

find-faults, as I will do yours, for upholding the nice fashion of
your country in denying me a kiss; therefore, patiently and
yielding. [*Kissing her.*] You have witchcraft in your lips, Kate.
There is more eloquence in a sugar touch of them than in the
tongues of the French Council; and they should sooner
persuade Harry of England than a general petition of monarchs.
Here comes your father.   260

Enter the FRENCH KING *and his* QUEEN, BURGUNDY,
and other Lords

BURGUNDY: God save your majesty. My royal cousin, teach
you our princess English?

KING HENRY: I would have her learn, my fair cousin, how
perfectly I love her; and that is good English.

BURGUNDY: Is she not apt?

KING HENRY: Our tongue is rough, coz, and my condition is
not smooth; so that, having neither the voice nor the heart of
flattery about me, I cannot so conjure up the spirit of love in
her, that he will appear in his true likeness.   269

BURGUNDY: Pardon the frankness of my mirth if I answer you
for that. If you would conjure in her, you must make a circle;
if conjure up love in her in his true likeness, he must appear
naked and blind. Can you blame her then, being a maid yet
rosed over with the virgin crimson of modesty, if she deny the
appearance of a naked blind boy in her naked seeing self? It
were, my lord, a hard condition for a maid to consign to.

KING HENRY: Yet they do wink and yield, as love is blind and
enforces.

BURGUNDY: They are then excused, my lord, when they see
not what they do.   280

KING HENRY: Then good my lord, teach your cousin to
consent winking.

BURGUNDY: I will wink on her to consent, my lord, if you will
teach her to know my meaning. For maids well summered and

285-6 *like . . . eyes*, like flies . . . sleepy and blundering though they can see.
285 *Bartholomew-tide*, 24 August.
286 *will endure handling*, (*a*) can be caught, (*b*) will accept love-making.
288-9 *This . . . summer*, the inference from this is that I must wait for a hot summer.

295 *perspectively*, i.e. through a glass cut to produce different pictures from different angles. Here the glass would show a maiden from one angle, a city from another.

300-1 *so . . . her*, may accompany her as her dowry.

302 *will*, i.e. the cities that he intended to have.

307 *firm proposed natures*, clearly stated conditions.
308 *Only . . . this*. Is this—an attempt to evade the issue, to show that Henry concedes nothing, a dramatic device to make it an impressive declaration?
310 *for . . . grant*, in connexion with grants of land or titles.

warm kept are like flies at Bartholomew-tide, blind, though they have their eyes; and then they will endure handling, which before would not abide looking on.

KING HENRY: This moral ties me over to time and a hot summer; and so I shall catch the fly, your cousin, in the latter end, and she must be blind too. 290

BURGUNDY: As love is, my lord, before it loves.

KING HENRY: It is so: and you may, some of you, thank love for my blindness, who cannot see many a fair French city for one fair French maid that stands in my way.

FRENCH KING: Yes my lord, you see them perspectively, the cities turned into a maid; for they are all girdled with maiden walls that war hath never entered.

KING HENRY: Shall Kate be my wife?

FRENCH KING: So please you. 299

KING HENRY: I am content, so the maiden cities you talk of may wait on her: so the maid that stood in the way for my wish shall show me the way to my will.

FRENCH KING: We have consented to all terms of reason.

KING HENRY: Is 't so, my lords of England?

WESTMORELAND: The King hath granted every article.
His daughter first, and then in sequel all,
According to their firm proposed natures.

EXETER: Only he hath not yet subscribed this: 308
Where your majesty demands, that the King of France, having any occasion to write for matter of grant, shall name your highness in this form and with this addition, in French, Notre très-cher fils Henri, Roi d'Angleterre, Héritier de France; and thus in Latin, Præclarissimus filius noster Henricus, Rex Angliæ, et Hæres Franciæ.

FRENCH KING: Nor this I have not, brother, so denied,
But your request shall make me let it pass.

KING HENRY: I pray you then, in love and dear alliance,
Let that one article rank with the rest,

237

324   *dear conjunction*, heartfelt union.
325   *neighbourhood*, neighbourliness.

335   *office*, dealing. *fell*, fierce.

337   *paction*, compact.

S.D.   A full ceremonial departure and with trumpet fanfare.

  And thereupon give me your daughter.   319
FRENCH KING: Take her fair son, and from her blood raise up
  Issue to me, that the contending kingdoms
  Of France and England, whose very shores look pale
  With envy of each other's happiness,
  May cease their hatred; and this dear conjunction
  Plant neighbourhood and christian-like accord
  In their sweet bosoms, that never war advance
  His bleeding sword 'twixt England and fair France.
ALL: Amen.
KING HENRY: Now welcome, Kate; and bear me witness all,
  That here I kiss her as my sovereign Queen.   [*Flourish*
QUEEN ISABEL: God, the best maker of all marriages,   331
  Combine your hearts in one, your realms in one.
  As man and wife being two, are one in love,
  So be there 'twixt your kingdoms such a spousal,
  That never may ill office, or fell jealousy,
  Which troubles oft the bed of blessed marriage,
  Thrust in between the paction of these kingdoms,
  To make divorce of their incorporate league;
  That English may as French, French Englishmen,
  Receive each other. God speak this Amen.   340
ALL: Amen.
KING HENRY: Prepare we for our marriage; on which day,
  My Lord of Burgundy, we'll take your oath,
  And all the peers', for surety of our leagues.
  Then shall I swear to Kate, and you to me;
  And may our oaths well kept and prosperous be.
                                          [*Sennet. Exeunt*

1-14 *Thus ... take.* A sonnet.

2   *bending*, (*a*) inadequate under the burden, (*b*) bowing.

4   *Mangling by starts*, spoiling by gaps and interruptions.

9   *bands*, baby-clothes.

11   *so ... managing*, i.e. disorder and divided leadership. See Intro-
     duction.

13   *oft ... shown. I Henry VI* was an extremely popular play.

14   *this acceptance take*, this play meet with your approval.
     For comment on this epilogue see Introduction, pp. 9, 19.

EPILOGUE

Enter Chorus

CHORUS: Thus far, with rough and all-unable pen,
    Our bending author hath pursued the story,
In little room confining mighty men,
    Mangling by starts the full course of their glory.
Small time, but in that small most greatly lived
    This star of England. Fortune made his sword,
By which the world's best garden he achieved,
    And of it left his son imperial lord.
Henry the Sixth, in infant bands crowned King
    Of France and England, did this King succeed;   10
Whose state so many had the managing,
    That they lost France, and made his England bleed;
Which oft our stage hath shown; and for their sake,
In your fair minds let this acceptance take.   *[Exit*

EPILOGUE

San Chiao

APPENDICES

I

SOURCES

THE historical elements in the play were taken mainly from Holinshed's *Chronicles*, 1587, but Shakespeare also drew from Hall's *Union of the Two Noble Families of Lancaster and York*, 1548, a work which also served as one of Holinshed's main sources. So close is the play to some parts of Holinshed, notably Canterbury's account of the Salic Law, that Shakespeare was probably working with a copy of the *Chronicles* open before him. His use of Hall is not so extensive, but numerous phrases show that Shakespeare was very familiar with Hall, particularly with Hall's emphasis on the need for unity. Some details in the play are thought to have come from early biographies and other chronicle histories. In short Shakespeare studied carefully the available material before writing the play.

Shakespeare's selection, and adaptation of his material give clues to his intentions. Admittedly none of this will be available to an audience in the theatre, but it is a valuable aid to a producer since it poses questions that help him to understand what the play is about.

The Prologue and the Choruses make it plain that many historical matters have had to be omitted owing to the limitations of space on the stage and the brief time taken by a performance. Thus five years elapse between the events of Act IV and those of Act V, but the gain in dramatic economy and energy is considerable. There are other changes of source-material which were intended to induce certain attitudes in the audience or to bring out certain themes. In the play it is Henry who makes demands on France and charges Canterbury to explain whether his claim to the French crown is valid or not. In Holinshed these matters were a 'sharp invention' of the churchmen to divert Henry's attention from the bill in Parliament. Again it is Henry not Westmoreland who raises the possibility of a Scottish invasion, and Henry commanded Exeter to 'use mercy on Harfleur', but according to Holinshed the town was sacked.

Not found in Hall or Holinshed are the boasting of the French nobles, Henry's incognito visit to his soldiers, the account of the deaths of York and Suffolk, Burgundy's description of the plight of France, Henry's speech before Harfleur. On the other hand Shakespeare omits all mention of the archers and their stakes at Agincourt.

Two episodes, the wooing scene and Pistol's capture of M. le Fer, the play has in common with an old play *The Famous Victories of Henry V*, acted before 1588, though Shakespeare's treatment is very different from that of his predecessor. It may be that the wooing was part of the Henry legend, but Shakespeare hints at profounder matters than the promise given in the epilogue to *2 Henry IV* to make his audience 'merry with fair Katharine of France'.

Shakespeare adds other episodes and incidents to the main story. Henry's pardon for the drunkard who had abused him, the trap set for the conspirators, the activities of the irregular humorists, Pistol, Bardolph, Nym, and the Boy, the account of Falstaff's death, the scene of the four nationals, the language lesson, Henry's conversation with his soldiers and the jest of the glove.

It is important to try to understand the dramatic reasons for these changes, and the function of the additions for however obscure and trivial they may seem they were not merely to tickle the ears of the groundlings.

II

SHAKESPEARE'S THEATRE

ALTHOUGH the evidence for the design of Elizabethan theatres is incomplete and conflicting, and although there were certainly differences of construction and arrangement, the following account, it is hoped, will give a reasonable outline.

The first public theatres in London were built during Shakespeare's lifetime. According to some they embodied in their design and construction the experience and practice of the medieval and Tudor play productions in inn yards, booth stages, and pageant wagons. Recently Glynne Wickham has argued strongly against this view, claiming that the game-houses, tournament arenas, banqueting chamber and town-hall

Courtesy of the British Council

MODEL OF AN ELIZABETHAN THEATRE
by Richard Southern

provide the basis for Elizabethan stages both public or in banqueting rooms (*Early English Stages*, II, Pt. 1, p. 267).

From square, circular or hexagonal theatre walls tiered with galleries for spectators, the Elizabethan stage jutted out over six feet above ground level and occupied about half the floor space where the spectators could stand on three sides of it. The stage of the Fortune theatre was 43 feet × 27 feet and the floor area in which it stood was 55 feet × 55 feet. At the back of the stage the lowest tier of spectators' galleries gave place to a curtained recess or inner stage, a study or discovery space, used for interior scenes. Another view is that there was no recess, but a curtained space under a canopy in front of the rear wall of the stage. On either side were dressing rooms from which entrance doors opened on to the stage. The first floor gallery behind the stage was used for scenes in the play; a second floor gallery or room was used by musicians. Above the balcony and covering the rear portion of the stage was a canopy or roof painted blue and adorned with stars sometimes supported by pillars from the stage. There were trap-doors in the stage and frequently a low rail around it.

The pillars, canopy, railings, and back stage were painted and adorned. If a tragedy was to be performed, the stage was hung with black, but there was no stage setting in the modern fashion.

There were stage properties usually of the kind that could be easily pushed on and off the stage. Records of the time mention a mossy bank, a wall, a bed, trees, arbours, thrones, tents, rock, tomb, hell-mouth, a cauldron; on the other hand tents, pavilions, and mansions may have been permanent 'sets' in some historical plays. These structures varied in size for a small one may have sufficed for the tomb in *Romeo and Juliet*, but the tent representing the Queen's chamber in Peele's *Edward I* contained six adults and a bed, as Armstrong pointed out. On the whole properties were limited to essentials although the popularity of the private masques with their painted canvas sets encouraged increasing elaboration of scenery and spectacle during the reign of James I.

There was no limitation to the display of rich and gorgeous costumes in the current fashion of the day. The more magnificent and splendid the better; indeed the costumes must have been the most expensive item in the requirements of the company. An occasional attempt was made at period costume, but normally plays were produced in Elizabethan garments without any suspicion of the oddness that strikes us when we read of Cæsar entering 'in his nightshirt' or Cleopatra calling on Charmian to cut the lace of what we may call her corsets. High rank was marked by magnificence of dress, a trade or calling by functional clothes. Feste, the clown, would wear the traditional fool's coat or petticoat of motley, a coarse cloth of mixed yellow and green. The coat was buttoned from the neck to the girdle from which hung a wooden dagger, its skirts voluminous with capacious pockets in which Feste might 'impetticoat' any 'gratillity'. Ghosts, who appear in a number of plays, wore a kind of leathern smock. Oberon and magicians such as Prospero wore, in the delightful phrase and spelling of the records, 'a robe for to goo invisibell'.

The actors formed companies under the patronage of noblemen for protection against a civic law condemning them as 'rogues, vagabonds and sturdy beggars' to severe punishment. They were the servants of their patron and wore his livery. The company was a co-operative society, its members jointly owned the property and shared the profits; thus Shakespeare's plays were not his to use as he liked, they belonged to his company, the Lord Chamberlain's Men. This company, honoured by James I when it became the King's Men, was the most successful company of the period. It had a number of distinguished actors, it achieved more Court performances than any other company, and it performed in the best London theatre, the Globe, until it was burnt down during a performance of *Henry VIII* in 1613. Women were not allowed on the public stage, although they performed in masques and theatricals in private houses. Boys, therefore, were apprenticed to the leading actors and took the female parts.

The audience in the public theatres was drawn from all classes. There were courtiers and inns of court men who appreciated intricate word play, mythological allusions, and the technique of sword play; there were the 'groundlings' who liked jigs, horse-play, and flamboyance of speech and spectacle; and there were the citizens who appreciated the romantic stories, the high eloquence of patriotic plays, and moral sentiments. A successful play would have something for all. Sometimes gallants would sit on a stool on the stage and behave rather like the courtiers in *A Midsummer Night's Dream*, V. i, or *Love's Labour's Lost*, V. ii. The 'groundlings' too were likely to be troublesome and noisy. They could buy bottled-beer, oranges, and nuts for their comfort; but it is noted to their credit that when Falstaff appeared on the stage, so popular was he that they stopped cracking nuts! They applauded a well delivered speech; they hissed a boring play; they even rioted and severely damaged one theatre. Shakespeare's plays however were popular among all classes: at Court they

> did so take Eliza and our James,

and elsewhere in the public theatre they outshone the plays of other dramatists. Any play of his was assured of a 'full house'. An ardent theatre-goer of the day praising Shakespeare's plays above those of other dramatists wrote:

> When let but Falstaff come,
> Hal, Poins, the rest, you scarce shall have a room,
> All is so pester'd; let but Beatrice
> And Benedick be seen, lo in a trice
> The cockpit, galleries, boxes, all are full
> To hear Malvolio, that cross-garter'd gull.

Shakespeare's Works

The year of composition of only a few of Shakespeare's plays can be determined with certainty. The following list is based on current scholarly opinion.

The plays marked with an asterisk were not included in the First Folio edition of Shakespeare's plays (1623) which was prepared by Heminge and Condell, Shakespeare's fellow actors. Shakespeare's part in them has been much debated.

1590–1   2 Henry VI, 3 Henry VI.
1591–2   1 Henry VI.
1592–3   Richard III, Comedy of Errors.
1593–4   Titus Andronicus, Taming of the Shrew, Sir Thomas More* (Part authorship. Four manuscript pages presumed to be in Shakespeare's hand).
1594–5   Two Gentlemen of Verona, Love's Labour's Lost, Romeo and Juliet, Edward III* (Part authorship).
1595–6   Richard II, A Midsummer Night's Dream.
1596–7   King John, Merchant of Venice, Love's Labour Won (Not extant. Before 1598).
1597–8   1 Henry IV, 2 Henry IV, The Merry Wives of Windsor.
1598–9   Much Ado About Nothing, Henry V.
1599–1600   Julius Caesar, As You Like It.
1600–1   Hamlet, Twelfth Night.
1601–2   Troilus and Cressida.
1602–3   All's Well that Ends Well.